CINDERS & SMOKE

A mile by mile guide for the Durango to Silverton narrow gauge trip

by

Doris B. Osterwald

author of

TICKET TO TOLTEC

A mile by mile guide® for the Cumbres and Toltec Scenic Railroad

and

ROCKY MOUNTAIN SPLENDOR

A mile by mile guide© for Rocky Mountain National Park

Western Guideways, Ltd.

P.O. Box 15532 · Lakewood. Colorado 80215

Printed by Golden Bell Press
Denver, Colorado

Color separations by LithoColor
Denver, Colorado

CONTENTS

Acknowledgements   4
Introduction
    General Information about Silverton Trains   6
    How to use Guide Maps   15
Mile by Mile Guide®   19
Historical Notes   59
For the Geologist   74
For the Naturalist   85
For the Railroader
    Engines   88
    Cars   96
    Track   109
Railroad Memorabilia
    Something Old   116
    Something New   130
Centennial Celebrations   132
The Restoration of Engine 480   134
Tragedy Strikes the Narrow Gauge   139
    Fire Destroys the Durango Roundhouse   142
    Work in the Open Air Roundhouse   146
Back on Track   148
References   149
Equipment Roster   151
Whistle Signals   inside back cover

ACKNOWLEDGEMENTS

A full head of steam was kept up for this book with the aid and encouragement of many friends, associates, and most of all my family. Special thanks must go to Misters H. F. Eno, Ed Roe and Alexis McKinney of the Denver and Rio Grande Western Railroad for engineering data sheets, specification drawings, and much help. In Durango, conductors Alva Lyons and Myron Henry, and trainman George Morgan gave much valuable information on the locations of snowslides and points of interest. Invaluable help on the research for this book was give by the staffs of the Colorado Historical Society, the Denver Public Library Western History Department, and the Durango Public Library. Special thanks are also due to Mr. Duncan Ross of Harold Walter Clark, Inc. of Denver for his help during all phases of the work. The cover was designed by Charles Zender, also of the Clark agency. Mr. Robert W. Richardson of the Colorado Railroad Museum generously read the railroading sections for accuracy. Other individuals whose help and encouragement I wish to acknowledge include Ellen and Wally Hansen, Doris and Les Nelson, Eleanor Muncey, Ernestine Mills, Elaine and Gene Sengelman, David Varnes, Jo Doubek, Maurice Reuler, James Forrest and Garland Neel.

(First Edition, June 1965)

In the 17 years since the first edition of Cinders & Smoke was published, many changes have taken place on **The Silverton** and history continues to be made. Many persons have helped to keep the book up to date. Jackson C. Thode, a primary source of railroad knowledge and lore, is always willing to answer questions. He spent many hours digging out details on the old coaches now being restored by the D&SNG. Richard E. Davis in the Engineering Department of the D&RGW graciously provided much data and drawings. New photographs and information have been unearthed, thanks to John Ison, Frances McCarthy and Elsie Neff of the Durango Public Library and to Dr. Robert W. Delaney, Catherine Conrad and Margarite Norton of the Center for Southwest Studies at Ft. Lewis College in Durango. My friend Bob Metzger has offered advice and support through the years and deserves a special "Thank you". To Bill Freeman of Sydney, Australia, many thanks for his yeoman service in reviewing various editions of Cinders & Smoke. His detailed notes and suggestions help make this edition much more accurate.

David V. Hughes, consulting engineer for KKBNA Company, Inc., graciously shared his photographs and experiences of that memorable day, August 7, 1981 when engine 481 made its first journey to Silverton. To Richard L. Hunter, a "Thank you" for his photographs and for his efforts to keep me informed of changes he found during his hikes down the Animas Canyon. Augie Mastroguiseppe of the Denver Public Library and Diane Radson of the Colorado Historical Society, were most helpful by seeing that photographs for the fourth edition were reproduced in time to meet deadlines. Yvonne Osterwald contributed the drawings of signs used along the railroad and redrafted the track profile.

To Charles E. Bradshaw, Jr., Amos Cordova and James M. Mayer, officers of the Durango & Silverton Narrow Gauge Railroad Company, my sincere thanks for their interest, help and encouragement in revising the book to cover the sale and first years's operation. **The Silverton** continues to have a very bright future!

The fourth edition of **Cinders & Smoke** was dedicated with deep gratitude to the countless, unnamed railroaders who in the past ran the engines, pounded the spikes, shovelled out the snowslides, repaired the track after floods and kept the rolling stock in good working order. Because of their hard work, people can continue to ride this authentic steam-powered train. Passengers will continue to be thrilled and awed at the sight of the Animas canyon gorge as the train inches along the High Line and to enjoy the ever-changing scenery in the beautiful San Juan Mountains.

As one who has been privileged to watch and record the events that have taken place on the Silverton Branch during the past 35 years, I believe 1981 and 1982 must be a high point in the long and colorful history of the line. That the railroad is still operating is amazing, considering the fates of all other Rocky Mountain narrow gauge railroads. **The Silverton** remains as a tribute to all those individuals whose efforts to save this 45-mile section of history were successful.

As the monument at Cascade Canyon wye states, the "Spirit of Colorado Mountain Railroading" is embodied in the narrow gauge track that follows the Animas River to Silverton. *(Fourth Edition, May 1982)*

Many pleasures and rewards come with an interest in railroading. In addition to the thrill of hearing a powerful steam engine working up a steep grade, the melodious sound of a whistle echoing across a canyon, or the dubious delight of having cinders and smoke land on one's face, the people met and the friends made are very special. The list grows with each passing year. To Joe Puliti, Paul Connor and Patsy Dolan of the D&SNG, very special thanks for all their help and support in arranging for this new edition. Paul's pictures are great additions, as are the ones taken by Eric Nelson two days after the roundhouse fire. Richard L. Hunter and Kenneth T. Gustafson, both model railroading friends, generously gave access to their large collections of pictures taken on many hiking trips into the Animas River canyon. Many thanks also to April Casale and my grandson Ren Osterwald who covered the special opening day festivities for me on May 5-6, 1989. *(Sixth Edition, May 1989)*

DBO

Durango depot, August 1985.   *(F. W. Osterwald)*

5

CINDERS & SMOKE

by
Doris B. Osterwald

INTRODUCTION

GENERAL INFORMATION ABOUT THE SILVERTON TRAINS

The train on which you ride is a relic of earlier years. The Silverton Branch was built in 1881-1882 by the Denver & Rio Grande Railway Company (D&RG) which started in Denver in 1870. By the end of 1882 the company operated trains over a thousand miles of track. Periods of bankruptcy and reorganizations were frequent in the company's history, however, and several name changes reflected these financial problems. In 1921, as the result of a major reorganization, the company became the present Denver & Rio Grande Western Railroad (D&RGW). Until the Silverton Branch was sold to the Durango & Silverton Narrow Gauge Railroad Company (D&SNG), the D&RGW operated this somewhat nostalgic means of transportation.

The schedules of the regular D&SNG trains are similar to those used by the D&RG in the early 1900's. Although operated primarily for visitors, schedules are rigidly maintained to the minute — without the benefit of speed recorders in the engine cabs! Today more convenient departure times from Durango and Silverton are scheduled, because connections with other trains at those points are no longer possible. The last connecting train — the D&RGW's San Juan, which was a daily deluxe train between Alamosa and Durango, was abandoned in 1951.

The D&SNG non-stop trains to Silverton (the first class San Juan Express) is No. 115 to Silverton and No. 116 to Durango. The original San Juan Express was the first D&RG through train from Denver to Salida, Colorado in 1880 when Salida was the end of the line. These trains, which normally offer extra-fare parlor car service, as well as regular passenger service, are direct descendants of the D&RG first class trains Nos. 15 and 16. In the 1886 timetable these trains, named the Silverton Accommodation, left Durango at 7:30 A.M. and arrived in Silverton at 12:40 P.M. By 1919 the first class trains were Nos. 115 and 116, named the San Juan and New Mexico Express, that left Durango at 5:50 P.M. after having originated in Alamosa, Colorado at 7:00 A.M. the same day.

The well-known Silverton passenger trains, No. 461 (the Silverton Mixed) to Silverton and No. 462 (the Durango Mixed) to Durango carry both passengers and freight. They bore these numbers at least as early as 1904 and were designated by the same names in the official 1919 timetable. The second mixed trains to Silverton were first operated as second sections of regularly scheduled trains Nos. 461 and 462 in 1963. When the second sections became officially scheduled, they were assigned Nos. 463 and 464. The

6

D&SNG named train 463 the **Second Silverton Mixed** and train 464 the **Second Durango Mixed** in 1982. These trains were joined by Nos. 465 and 466 in 1986. Nos. 461, 463 and 465 then were named the **Silverton Mixed** and Nos. 462, 464 and 466 became the **Durango Mixed.** In your passengers' timetables all these trains are called the First, Second and Third Silverton Trains. Freight on mixed trains is carried in two boxcars painted "Rio Grande Gold" to match the coaches. If the volume of freight is too great for the yellow boxcars, extra freights are operated.

Other D&SNG trains have no obvious origins in former Rio Grande schedules. The **Cascade Canyon Mixed,** when operated in the winter between Durango and Cascade Canyon wye, bore Nos. 261 and 262. During the summers, trains No. 265 (northbound) and No. 266 (southbound), also named the **Cascade Canyon Mixed,** run between Durango and Cascade Canyon wye in the late afternoon and evening. These trains offer extra-fare parlor car service in addition to regular coach seats.

The total running time for all trains is less than shown by old schedules because there still are fewer trains over the track, and fewer and shorter stops are necessary. All mixed trains make informal stops to let off and pick up fishermen, campers, hikers, photographers and mountaineer climbers with their equipment. Express trains stop only for water.

Travelers who rode **The Silverton** in the early 1950's or before will miss one touch of informality, however. The traditional D&RGW Silverton Branch caboose, with the conductor's over-sized coffee pot, was taken off the train as a passenger safety measure. In contrast, a modern radio communications system was added in 1981. Also in 1981, a train dispatcher began to work at the Durango depot for the first time in over 30 years. All movements on the line, including motor cars and light engines, now require permission from the Durango dispatcher.

Operating rules on the D&SNG are adhered to as rigidly as on any standard gauge main-line road, as shown by the classification flags and lights placed on the locomotive and by the marker lights carefully hung on the last car by the trainman each morning (photo, page 99). These flags and lights are not mere decorations — to railroaders they have definite meanings. For example, the locomotive of a regularly scheduled train with no following section carries no flags or lighted marker lamps. The locomotive of the first section of a two-section train will carry green classification flags and marker lights, but the locomotive of the following section will carry no flags or lights. The locomotive of an extra (or unscheduled) train will carry white flags and lights. Red marker lights or flags on the rear car indicate that the assembled equipment is an authorized train with operating rights, and tell track-side observers that the train is intact and has not broken in two. The locomotive headlights are always turned on while trains are operating. These also serve as signals; when a train enters a siding to allow another train to pass, the headlight of the waiting engine is turned off to let the other engineer know that the entire train is in the siding and that the mainline is clear.

A small red indicator on a long steel rod attached to the right side of the smoke-box front of the locomotive, is a signal to the engineer that the flanger chisels under the locomotive pilot are up or down. These chisels, which are used to clear ice and packed snow from inside both rails in winter so that there is enough clearance for the wheel flanges, must be raised while crossing roads and traveling through switches or guardrails.

7

Motorists arriving in Durango in the late afternoon or evening may become aware of the D&SNG Railroad as a train whistles loud and clear for crossings of the Durango streets after its downhill run along the Animas River. A whistle is not just a noisemaker; it is used by the engineer to give signals of movements the train is about to make. In general, these signals announce starting, stopping, backing up, approaching road crossings and stations, serve as warnings to persons or livestock on or near the track and inform trainmen protecting the front or rear of stopped trains to reboard. The most common whistle signals are given on the inside back cover. The bell is also used as a signal. It is rung as a warning when the train is about to leave or approach a station and serves as an additional warning signal at major road crossings.

If you ride in a closed coach, it may have been built as early as 1879, or as late as 1963 or 1964 to earlier specifications (see pages 96-109). Interiors of the older cars look very much as they did in the 1880's, except that carpeting has been replaced with linoleum and the overstuffed plush seats replaced with bus seats, mostly from the Denver Tramway Corp. Coal stoves are still used to heat the coaches in winter or on cold, rainy days. Cars rebuilt by the D&SNG are carefully insulated for winter operations (see photos, page 103). The open cars were rebuilt from standard gauge cars by the D&RGW and by the D&SNG (see pages 105-106).

Take a quick look at the track. Not only do the rails look small, as compared to modern main-line railroads, but they are also closer together. The rails weigh a minimum of 85 pounds per yard — compared to the 100 to 136 pounds per yard on heavily traveled standard gauge main-lines. (See page 109 and profile, page 110). The distance between the rails (gauge) is only 3 feet instead of the 4 feet 8½ inches on standard gauge lines. These 85 pound rails, small as they are, would seem large if compared to the 30 pound rails that were used when the line was built in 1881-1882. Today's sawed and creosoted ties, even though shorter for narrow gauge use than standard gauge ties, would seem quite sophisticated if they were compared with the untreated rough-hewn ties of the 1880's (photo, page 66).

The track switches in use today are different from the original ones. The old type, called stub switches, were simply devices that moved the running rails from one position to another. Today's switches consist of fixed running rails with a pair of knife-shaped tapered points that can be moved from one side to the other between the rails. A switch stand is located at each track switch. A vertical steel rod with a handle that is connected to a crank pushes a rod between the ties to move the switch points from one side to the other. On top of the vertical rod is a green metal diamond and directly below is a round red metal **Switch Stand** target placed at right angles to the diamond. The engineer will see the green diamond if the switch is aligned for the main track, or the red circle if it is aligned for the diverging or side track.

The engine of your train (see pages 88-95) will be a 2-8-2 (Mikado) type of one of three classes of steam locomotives owned by the D&SNG. These engines all bear the same numbers and class designations that they did when owned by the D&RGW. Steam locomotives are classified by the arrangements of their wheels and the amount of tractive effort available. A 2-8-2 engine has a 2-wheel pilot truck, 8 drive wheels and a 2-wheel trailing truck under the cab.

8

Ten engines of the 470-Series, Class K-28 (the K stands for Mikado) were built by the American Locomotive Co. in New York in 1923 for the D&RGW. Only three of these engines still exist (Nos. 473, 476 and 478) and all are owned by the D&SNG. Two 480-Series, Class K-36 engines owned by the D&SNG (Nos. 480 and 481) are part of a group of ten built for the D&RGW by the Baldwin Locomotive Works in Philadelphia, Pa. in 1925. The D&SNG also owns four 490-Series, Class K-37 locomotives (Nos. 493, 497, 498 and 499) which were built for the D&RG by Baldwin in 1902 as standard gauge 2-8-0's (D&RG Class C-41). In 1928 and 1930, ten of the C-41's were rebuilt in Denver at the Burnham Shops of the Rio Grande as narrow gauge 2-8-2's with new frames and wheels supplied by Baldwin.

The three classes of active D&RGW narrow gauge locomotives were steamed up and ready to work when this photograph was taken in September, 1968 at the Durango roundhouse.

(R. W. Osterwald)

The original locomotives used on the Silverton Branch were much smaller than the 470-Series. They consisted of 2-8-0 (Consolidation) types, which were smaller than D&RGW 315 on display at the Durango Chamber of Commerce, and an assortment of even smaller and lighter 2-6-0 (Mogul) and 4-6-0 (Ten-wheeler) types. The heaviest of the early 2-8-0 engines weighed only 37 tons and pulled with 18,947 pounds of effort; the other locomotives exerted even less tractive effort. For comparison, a K-28 engine pulls with 27,500 pounds of effort. Labor was cheap in 1882, however, and the D&RG simply ran more and shorter trains or used more helper engines.

A close look at an engine standing at the station will reveal several unusual features. The front of the K-28 (470-Series) engines (the smoke box) is adorned by an odd-shaped collection of machinery and pipes known as a compound air pump (compressor). Similar pumps hang under the running boards (walk-ways) of the K-36 (480's) and K-37 (490's) engines. These pumps are operated by steam from the boiler, and provide compressed air to operate the brakes on the entire train and other equipment on the engine. The long tanks hung beneath the running boards are reservoirs to store the compressed air. Another small cylinder on the right side of the engine beneath the running board and just ahead of the cab on engine 478 (photo, page 93) is a steam-powered device used to reverse valves in the cylinders so that the engine can run backwards. Only a few D&RGW narrow gauge engines were equipped with these power reverses. Mounted on top of the boiler just ahead of the cab is a steam-powered electric generator (identified by its upward curved exhaust pipe) which is used to operate lights and radio equipment. The rounded dome on top of the boiler nearest the cab is used to store steam under pressure for the cylinders and to operate the whistle. It also contains the throttle valve. The second dome contains sand used for extra traction when the rails are slippery.

Coupled behind the locomotive is a tender which carries 5,000 gallons of water for a K-28 or K-36 engine, or 6,000 gallons for a K-37 engine. The tender also holds 8 tons of soft coal for a K-28, 9.5 tons for a K-36 or 9 tons for a K-37 engine. Coal and water are the ingredients that make a steam engine move. The fireman, who sits on the left-hand side of the engine, shovels coal from the tender into the firebox through a large door in the center of the cab. Water is pumped from the tender into the boiler where burning coal in the firebox heats the water to make steam. The fireman is also responsible to see that there is enough water in the boiler to prevent damage to the engine. The steam expands in the cylinders (located low on each side of the engine near the front) to push the pistons which are connected to the wheels by means of the rods.

One of the most interesting features on the locomotives are the wheel assemblies (called running gear). A look under the running board of an engine reveals that the drive wheels are actually inside the frame of the locomotive, rather than outside. The axles extend outward past the wheels and through the frame to the counterweights, which are attached to the axle ends. These counterweights are parts of the wheels on the more common inside-frame steam locomotives. The side and main rods are connected to the outside counterweights along with the valve operating rods (photo, page 11). The fronts of the main rods are pivoted on the cross-heads. The cross-heads are attached to the rear ends of the piston rods which are shoved back and forth by steam entering the cylinders. The motions made by all these moving parts are fascinating to watch when the engine moves.

When new, all of the locomotives now owned by the D&SNG had straight smoke stacks, to which the D&RGW added cap-shaped cinder catchers as precautions against fire (photos, pages 92, 93). The first order of business for the D&SNG in 1981 was to remove the fake diamond stacks which had been added to the K-28 engines in 1956 for a movie (photo, page 11. These stacks, however, had been on the engines for almost half of their lives. False coal-oil headlights and wooden pilots (cowcatchers) had previously been removed.

Brakes on trains are operated by air pressure. The most obvious features of the air brake system on the train are the large rubber hoses beneath the couplers on each car and on the engine. These hoses are connected to pipes beneath the cars to form a continuous air line from the engine to the rear car of the train. The air pressure for the brake system is provided by the air compressor on the engine. The air brakes, however, operate differently from

Running gear of the 476, showing rods, valve gear and outside counterweights. Cooling pipes and air tank are just below the running board. The fake diamond stack, added for a movie in 1956, was removed by D&SNG RR in 1981.   (F. W. Osterwald)

the brakes on an automobile which work by **increasing** the pressure in the system when the brake pedal is pressed. About 70 to 90 pounds per square inch of air pressure are maintained in the air line while the train is moving. When the engineer operates his brake lever, air pressure in the line is **reduced,** causing cylinders on each car to force the brake shoes against the wheels to slow the train. If the air line develops a leak or is broken, the brakes will "go into emergency" and stop the train automatically until the air line is repaired and the air pressure allowed to build up. An air gauge in the engine tells the engineer how much pressure is in the brake system. The rear car normally has an air pressure gauge as well. Large steel handwheels on each car are used to lock the brakes by hand when cars are stored, much like the parking brake on an automobile. The narrow gauge D&RG was the first U.S. railroad to have air brakes on both freight and passenger equipment.

Milepost

During your trip you probably will notice a number of small track-side signals, in addition to the switchstands. The most common of these are the mileposts. Their history and use are described on page 15 and on the back cover. Other signals tell the engineer when to whistle or warn him of a road crossing. Yard limits (boundaries beyond which no train movements can be made without orders from the dispatcher) are marked by signs

11

Whistle

Crossing

Yard Limit

Raise Flanger

with two blades angled upward. These will be found near Durango, Ah Wilderness, and Silverton. Another common trackside signal is a small black equilateral triangle with two horizontal white lines. This sign tells the engineer to raise the air-operated ice chisels on the small, heavy car called a flanger during snow clearing operations, as well as to raise the flanger chisels on his engine. You may also see a large metal blue sign (flag) attached to the engine after it is coupled to the train at the Durango depot. This blue flag tells the engineer that carmen are working around or under the train. Until this sign is removed by an authorized supervisor, the train is not permitted to move.

If you are fortunate enough to ride the train after a heavy snow, a work train with a large steel plow on the locomotive pilot and pulling a flanger (see photo, page 134) will precede the passenger train to clear snow from the track. The flanger chisels and the blades that push the snow away from the track are operated by air pressure from the locomotive. A round, red target on the flanger, resembling the red target on a switch stand, tells the engineer whether the chisels are up or down. Road engines on wintertime passenger trains routinely carry snowplows on the pilots.

None of the D&SNG locomotives carry speed recorders. In order to maintain schedules, the engineers must use their watches to time the rate at which they pass mileposts, road crossings, bridges, prominent rocks and notable trees. By comparing these times with a speed table, they know how fast they are traveling. Engineers also judge speed by the sound of the engine exhaust — four exhausts per revolution of the wheels. The rhythm gives them the speed.

SPEED TABLE		
If the train passes between mileposts in:		**Then the speed is:**
3 Minutes	0 Seconds	20 MPH
3	30	17.1
4	0	15
4	30	14.1
5	0	12
5	30	10.9
6	0	10

These speed-determining techniques have been used since the early days of railroading and have a lot of practical value. The Denver & Rio Grande Railway Employees Timetable No. 19, effective July 23, 1882, contained the permanent restriction that "No train or engine must use less than twenty (20) minutes running between Rockwood and Animas River Bridge, three miles west of Rockwood." This locality is the High Line, and a slow order is still in effect restricting trains to a maximum of 8 miles per hour.

This historic photo was taken in Silverton August 7, 1981 when engine 481 and a caboose arrived for the first time. On the train were D&S officials and David V. Hughes, who was responsible for the engineering work done to upgrade the track and bridges. The Silverton Mixed, double-headed by engines 476 and 478 is standing on the first track.

(David V. Hughes)

Engine 478 passing the Silverton wye with southbound train No. 464. As soon as the train cleared the switch, the brakeman realigned the switch so 481 and its caboose could return to Durango.

(David V. Hughes)

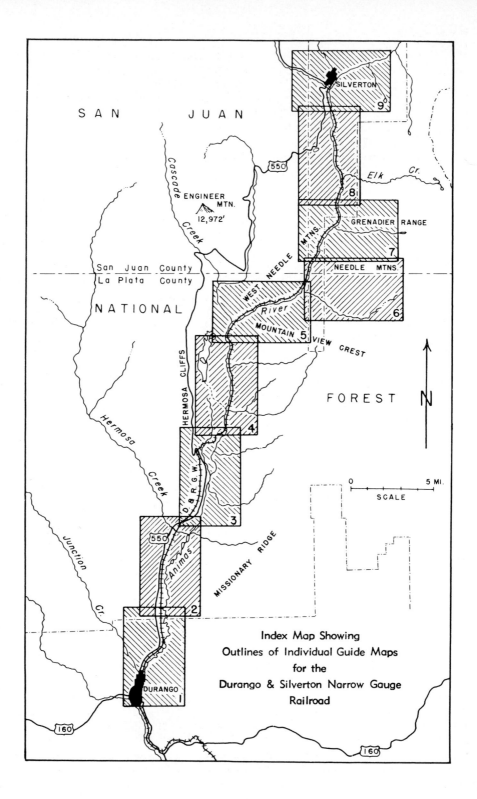

S A N   J U A N

Cascade Creek

ENGINEER MTN.
12,972'

San Juan County
La Plata County

N A T I O N A L

SILVERTON

9

550

Elk Cr.

8

GRENADIER RANGE

7

WEST NEEDLE MTNS.

NEEDLE MTNS.

6

River

MOUNTAIN 5

VIEW CREST

Hermosa Creek

HERMOSA CLIFFS

F O R E S T

N

4

D & R G W

3

Animas

MISSIONARY RIDGE

550

Junction Cr.

2

0   5 MI.
SCALE

1

DURANGO

Index Map Showing
Outlines of Individual Guide Maps
for the
Durango & Silverton Narrow Gauge
Railroad

160

160

14

HOW TO USE THE GUIDE MAPS

The spectacular scenery along this 45 miles of railroad track is the sum total of erosion of the landforms by running water, glacial ice and wind, coupled with the opposite forces of nature, mountain building or uplift. The layers of rock that are tilted upward toward Silverton and disappear beneath the surface between mileposts 454 and 466 offer stark evidence of these mountain building forces at work. The high peaks of the Needle Mountains and the Grenadier Range stood as sentinels (monadnocks) over the lower mountains that were covered with ice and snow during past glacial periods.

Like the pages in a book, the rock layers are deposited one upon another with many interruptions (erosion and glaciation), so that while the record of geologic history is fairly easy to decipher, it is far from complete. The geology as shown on the guide maps has been generalized and as few technical terms as possible are used. A glossary of terms used is given on page 81. For the geologist, there is a complete geologic column on page 76 and a brief account of the geologic history of the Animas canyon area. Nature has carved the Animas canyon and exposed the many different rocks to be seen on this trip; the geologists named these rock layers (called formations) and devised the method of illustrating them on maps. The formation names represent mappable units that can be traced from one locality to another. In this guide many formations are grouped together into map units for simplicity. See List of Rocks on page 17 or the complete columnar section on page 76. The direction and degree of dip of the rocks from the horizontal plane is not shown on the guide maps. The maps show the entire name of the rock units when possible, otherwise a standard geological abbreviation is used. The letters Q,T,K,P,D, C or pre- C indicate the geologic age of the map unit, and the letter following is usually the first letter of the name of the major formation in the unit. For example, Qm is the abbreviation for a Quaternary moraine deposit, K is used for Cretaceous rocks, and Ph indicates the Hermosa Group of rocks of Pennsylvanian age.

Equally important parts of the landscape are the trees and flowers. It would be a dull trip without the shiny scrub oak leaves shining in the sun, the lush aspen groves, the stately blue spruce along the water's edge, or hillsides of yellow rabbitbrush blooming in the fall. Because more than 5000 species of plants grow in the Rocky Mountain region, only the most common and easiest seen trees, shrubs, and flowers are pointed out in the guide. For the naturalist, there is a brief discussion of the Life Zones in Colorado and a list of the common flowers, trees, animals and birds in each zone. The diagram on page 87 shows the changes in elevation from Durango to Silverton, the two life zones and how they overlap.

The text to accompany the nine guide maps is keyed to the mileposts found along the east side of the railroad track, and to the U.S. Forest Service signs on each side of the track. The mileposts are steel posts set about 10 to 20 feet out from the track with the numbers visible from two directions. The numbers indicate the distance by rail from Denver where the D&RG started. On the maps, each mile between mileposts is divided into tenths to aid in following map and text. All points of interest are described as being either **east** or **west** of the railroad track. For locations up or down the track, the direction is first given for the trip **to** Silverton, and the direction in brackets ( ) is for the return trip. An explanation of the symbols used on the maps is found on pages 16 and 17. The top of each map is north.

15

EXPLANATION OF SYMBOLS USED ON GUIDE MAPS

 Narrow guage railroad track. Number in box shows location of milepost along east side of track, and indicates the distance in miles by rail from Denver where the D. & R. G. started. Cross-ties are one-tenth of a mile apart to aid in following map and text. Fine line indicates abandoned railroad.

 Animas River and tributary streams.

 Boundary between rocks, with symbol for name of the rock type or formation. Dashed lines indicate indistinct boundaries (contacts).

Fault. Dashed where inferred.

Mineralized fault.

Andesite and / or latite dike.

Mineralized dike.

Mineral vein.

⚒ 14   Old mine or prospect. Numbers indicate mine referred to in text.

ARROW PEAK
13, 803'   High peaks, some of which can be seen from the train.

■
Tacoma   Railroad station.

 Major snowslide area.

Old toll or wagon road.

●   Water tank.

[550]   U. S. Highway.

Lake.

Railroad bridge.

County boundary.

Heavy dashed lines at top and bottom of guide maps indicates overlap of maps.

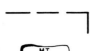 Point of interest sign erected by the U. S. Forest Service.

LIST OF ROCKS ON GUIDE MAPS

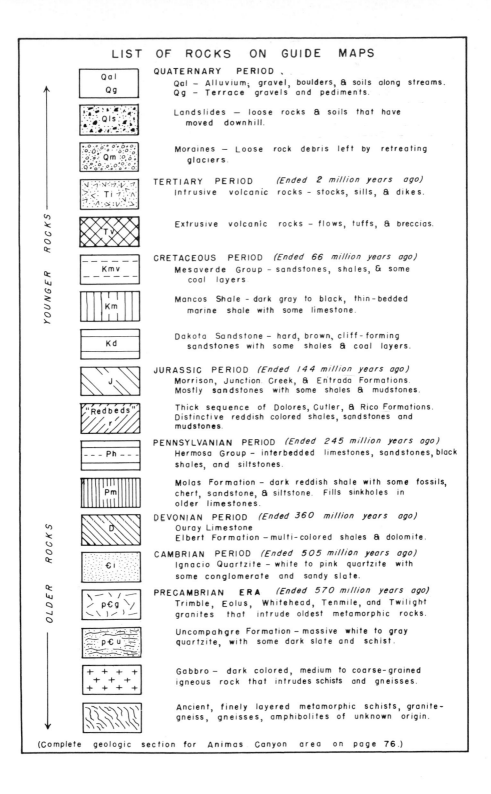

YOUNGER ROCKS

OLDER ROCKS

QUATERNARY PERIOD
Qal – Alluvium; gravel, boulders, & soils along streams.
Qg – Terrace gravels and pediments.

Landslides — loose rocks & soils that have moved downhill.

Moraines — Loose rock debris left by retreating glaciers.

TERTIARY PERIOD *(Ended 2 million years ago)*
Intrusive volcanic rocks - stocks, sills, & dikes.

Extrusive volcanic rocks - flows, tuffs, & breccias.

CRETACEOUS PERIOD *(Ended 66 million years ago)*
Mesaverde Group - sandstones, shales, & some coal layers

Mancos Shale - dark gray to black, thin-bedded marine shale with some limestone.

Dakota Sandstone - hard, brown, cliff-forming sandstones with some shales & coal layers.

JURASSIC PERIOD *(Ended 144 million years ago)*
Morrison, Junction Creek, & Entrada Formations. Mostly sandstones with some shales & mudstones.

Thick sequence of Dolores, Cutler, & Rico Formations. Distinctive reddish colored shales, sandstones and mudstones.

PENNSYLVANIAN PERIOD *(Ended 245 million years ago)*
Hermosa Group - interbedded limestones, sandstones, black shales, and siltstones.

Molas Formation - dark reddish shale with some fossils, chert, sandstone, & siltstone. Fills sinkholes in older limestones.

DEVONIAN PERIOD *(Ended 360 million years ago)*
Ouray Limestone
Elbert Formation — multi-colored shales & dolomite.

CAMBRIAN PERIOD *(Ended 505 million years ago)*
Ignacio Quartzite - white to pink quartzite with some conglomerate and sandy slate.

PRECAMBRIAN ERA *(Ended 570 million years ago)*
Trimble, Eolus, Whitehead, Tenmile, and Twilight granites that intrude oldest metamorphic rocks.

Uncompahgre Formation — massive white to gray quartzite, with some dark slate and schist.

Gabbro — dark colored, medium to coarse-grained igneous rock that intrudes schists and gneisses.

Ancient, finely layered metamorphic schists, granite-gneiss, gneisses, amphibolites of unknown origin.

(Complete geologic section for Animas Canyon area on page 76.)

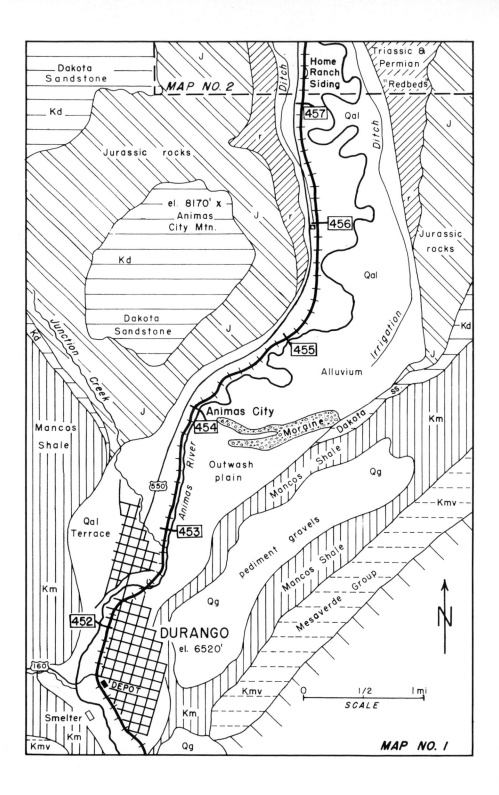

Milepost No. 451.5 **DURANGO DEPOT.** Welcome aboard the **Durango & Silverton's** narrow gauge train for an unforgettable "trip to yesterday." About 15 minutes before the "All aboard" call is given, the engine puffs off the ready track near the roundhouse, rolls north past the string of waiting cars, is switched onto track No. 1, or No. 2 and backs down to the train. A gentle (?) bump or two indicates the engine is coupled. The conductor gives the final "All aboard" and the train starts to roll. The track crosses U.S. 160 and goes north through the business section of Durango along Narrow Gauge Avenue.

Milepost No. 452.0 **CORNER, NARROW GAUGE AVE. AND 11th STREET.** Safeway store is on the southwest corner. In the lively 1880's, Durango's sporting houses were west of the track on 10th and 11th Streets. The "shady ladies" houses had such names as Bessie's, Jennie's, Mattie's, the Variety Theater, Clipper, Silver Bell, and the Hanging Gardens of Babylon. To the west is a good view of Perin's Peak, named for Charles Perin who surveyed the Durango townsite.

Milepost No. 452.2 **TRACK CROSSES MAIN STREET.** Picking up speed, the engine whistles loud and clear before the train crosses the street. Nostalgic cinders, coal smoke, and whistles will become a part of your day!

Milepost No. 452.4 **CROSS ANIMAS RIVER.** (See page 59). The bridge is 253 feet long and consists of a steel plate girder span brought from the Pleasant Valley Branch in Utah in 1927, a steel Pratt truss span built in 1888 and brought from the Conejos River near Antonito in 1917, and a wooden open-deck truss span built in 1936. The original bridge, built in 1881, was partially washed away during a spring flood in 1885. A state fish hatchery is west of the track. There is a good view of the La Plata Mountains to the northwest. The houses to the east are on a river terrace of gravel. Behind the terrace is a cliff of soft gray to black Mancos Shale, which was deposited as mud in a sea 90 million years ago. The material in the terrace is loose gravel, boulders, and soil which was dumped originally by retreating glaciers of the Late Wisconsin Stage about 17 thousand years ago. Since then the river has cut down through this loose material to its present channel. On the skyline is Perin's Peak, which is capped by tan to dirty rusty brown sandstone ledges of the Mesaverde Group that were deposited near the shore of the old sea. Coal beds associated with these sandstones were mined at Perin's Peak, as well as near Durango.

Milepost No. 452.85 **CROSS JUNCTION CREEK.** This creek joins the Animas from the northwest.

Milepost No. 453.0 **TRACK ALONG THE RIVER.** Wildflowers include Rocky Mountain iris, sand lilies, tiny white daisies, the ever-present dandelion in the spring; primrose, locoweed, sunflowers, and harebells in the summer months, and purple asters, yellow composites, and cattails in the fall.

Milepost No. 453.6 **PIPE LINES CROSS RIVER.** The houses on the flat surface east of the river are on a large glacial moraine.

Milepost No. 453.95 **TRACK CROSSES 32nd STREET, ANIMAS CITY.** Thirty-Second street crosses the river and follows along the base of a group of low, hummocky hills which are the terminal moraine of the Late Wisconsin glacial ice. A terminal moraine is the place where the

Engine 481 ready to leave Durango in September, 1981, with train No. 461, the Silverton Mixed. Engineer Mark Yeamans was conferring with Conductor Fred Paulek and Trainmaster George Connor. *(D. B. Osterwald)*

Train No. 261 at Durango, February, 1982. Engineer Richard Braden was waiting for the blue flag to be removed before leaving for Cascade Canyon wye. *(D. B. Osterwald)*

glacier stopped moving downstream, deposited its accumulated debris, and retreated. These rounded irregular hills are best seen on the return trip.

Milepost No.
454.3 **TRACK CROSSES 36th STREET.** Railroad grade is cut through the moraine here.

Milepost No.
454.9 **CLIFFS ABOVE TRAILER COURT** on west side of the track are thick, rusty brown and light tan layers of the Dakota Sandstone (Kd on map) at the top, which were deposited as sand in a sea about 100 million years ago; in the center the multi-colored shales, mudstones, and sandstones of the Morrison Formation, which were deposited as sand and mud by rivers and lakes about 150 million years ago; and at the base the massive, white to buff colored sandstone of the Entrada Formation which was deposited by wind in ancient dunes about 160 million years ago. The Morrison and Entrada are shown together on Map No. 1 as "J". As the train goes up the valley, notice the gently tilted sedimentary rocks gradually disappearing beneath the surface; these same rocks are deeply buried in the San Juan Basin of northwest New Mexico. Although some oil is produced from the Dakota and Hermosa Formations in the Basin, most is from sandstones of the Mesaverde Group (found at 4400 to 5500 feet depth) and the Pictured Cliffs Formation (2000 to 3400 feet depth).

Milepost No.
455.0 **SHARP BEND IN RIVER CHANNEL MEETS TRACK.** The lowest, massive, buff-colored sandstone cliff above U.S. 550 and across the valley is the Entrada Formation, included in unit "J" on

Milepost No. Map No. 1, which dips beneath the surface at M.P. 455.5.
455.9 **UNITED CAMPGROUND.**

Milepost No.
456.0 **IRON HORSE RESORT.** The tree-covered slopes on both sides of the valley are capped by the Dakota Sandstone (Kd on map). A good close-up view of the emerging (disappearing) "redbeds" is due west of the Resort. The bright red and rusty red shales and thin sandstone layers of the Dolores Formation, which were deposited by rivers in an ancient desert about 170 to 187 million years ago, are 400 to 600 feet thick here. Between Durango and Rockwood, the train passes from relatively young rocks to older crystalline rocks. The Animas River meanders back and forth across the valley floor between mileposts 454 and 465, and has formed many cut-off meanders and ox-bow lakes by cutting new, shorter channels between narrow looping bends of the river. As the river continued to carve away the valley floor, the curving lakes and cut-off meanders were isolated. The Animas winds its way back and forth across this wide valley because the low stream gradient was established by the glaciers and not by the river itself. Track goes through thick willow grove. Other shrubs along here include chokecherry, snowberry, buffaloberry, and box elder. In the fall the clematis vines have a fuzz of feathery seed tails hanging on the shrubs and trees. This fuzz was used by the Indians to start fires because a spark struck from flint or pyrite was quickly ignited. This material was also used to insulate boots and moccasins against the cold.

Milepost No.
457.2 **HOME RANCH SIDING.** 1000 feet long. Built in 1982 to handle increased traffic. Home Ranch spur was originally at M.P. 457.86.

Milepost No.
457.5 **GOOD VIEWS ON BOTH SIDES OF THE VALLEY** of the "redbeds" (labeled "r" on maps) which have a total thickness of about 2500 feet. In addition to the Dolores Formation at the top, there are 1900 feet of the Cutler Formation, and 100 to 165 feet of the Rico Formation at the base. These redbeds were deposited as sand and mud

21

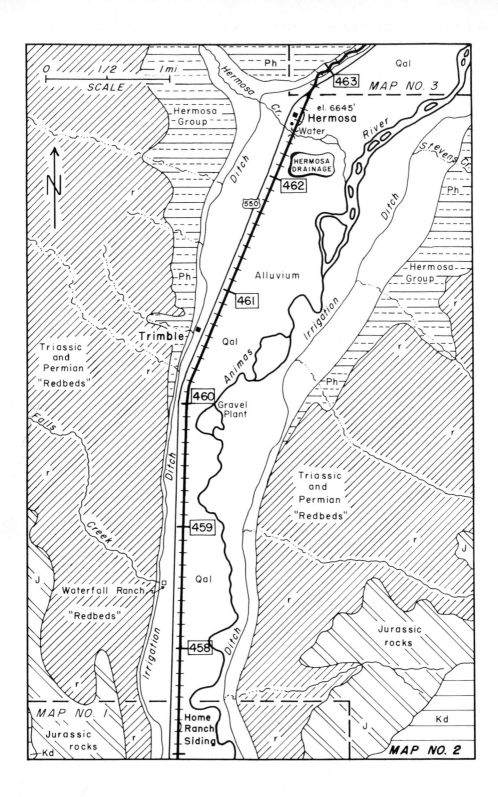

SCALE 0 1/2 1 mi.

N

Hermosa Group

Ph

Qal

463 MAP NO. 3

el. 6645' Hermosa

Water

HERMOSA DRAINAGE

462

550

Stevens Cr.

Ph

Ditch

River

Hermosa Cr.

Ditch

Hermosa Group

Alluvium

461

Irrigation

r

Ph

r

Trimble

Qal

Animas

r

460

Gravel Plant

Triassic and Permian "Redbeds"

r

Falls

459

Qal

Triassic and Permian "Redbeds"

r

r

J

Creek

r

J

Waterfall Ranch

"Redbeds"

Qal

458

Ditch

Jurassic rocks

r

J

Kd

Irrigation

MAP NO. 1

Jurassic rocks

Home Ranch Siding

r

J

Kd

Kd

MAP NO. 2

22

by rivers flowing across an ancient desert from 187 to 208 million years ago. The red color is formed when magnetite, an iron-bearing mineral, rusts and the resulting minerals — hematite and limonite — coat the sand grains and cement that make up the rock. Potato Hill, locally called Spud Mountain, is due north and was named for Potato John Raymond, a favorite cook on some early geological surveys of the west.

Milepost No. 458.5 **WATERFALL ON CLIFF TO WEST OF TRACK.** Falls Creek flows off layers of the Cutler Formation. The ranch, just east of the falls, is named Waterfall and is one of the oldest in the valley. It was started by Thomas H. Wigglesworth, Superintendent of Construction on the Silverton Branch of the D&RG.

Milepost No. 459.0 **FIRST VIEW OF MOUNTAIN VIEW CREST TO THE NORTH-EAST.** Many better views of the range will be visible farther up the canyon.

Milepost No. 460.0 **MILEPOST IS NEAR HOUSE.** Flowers here include silver sage, clover, butter and eggs, clematis vines, thistles, Indian paintbrush, goldenrod, and cattails. Cattail is a plant of many uses. The leaves are used for weaving, the brown flowers can be used for tinder in starting a fire, in bouquets, or when separated, the fuzz can be used for insulation or bedding. The lower stem and roots contain nearly pure starch that can be eaten either cooked or raw. The cores of the large rootstocks were dried and ground into meal by the Indians and early settlers. Muskrat, geese, and elk like to feed on the rootstocks and new shoots. The abundant thin-leaved willows have small yellow catkins in the early summer.

Milepost No. 460.69 **TRIMBLE HOT SPRINGS.** To the west at the base of the hill was a resort which was popular for many years. There was a siding and small depot here years ago. Plans were first announced for building a resort hotel on March 25, 1882, and the formal opening was held December 28, 1882 with a grand ball. Regular excursion trains stopped here; fare from Durango to Trimble was $1.00. There was also a bicycle path from Durango. Water for the swimming pools flowed from two hot springs at the rate of 150 to 200 gallons per minute. The temperature of the water was from 90° to 126° F.

Ernest Ingersoll, a reporter for the New York Tribune, wrote in 1885 of the resort:

> "A capacious hotel, of attractive exterior and admirably arranged and furnished within, affords the comforts of a home. Nearby is a bath-house one hundred feet in length, and equipped in the most approved modern style, with all varieties of baths."

Fire destroyed the main building in 1963, and the resort closed. *

Milepost No. 461.3 **IN THE LEDGES WEST OF THE HIGHWAY** is the contact between the red Rico Formation and gray and rusty brown shales and limestones of the Hermosa Group. The Hermosa was deposited as limy mud in the sea about 270 million years ago. It contains many fossils of marine animals.

Milepost No. 462.0 **HERMOSA DRAINAGE SIGNPOST.** The Animas valley from Durango to Baker's Bridge, east of milepost 466, is a broad U-shaped valley in which the river meanders back and forth across lush meadows.

Many wildflowers grow here. The 2- to 4-foot tall, coarse, woolly spiked plant that has small yellow flowers at the top is mullein. It blooms in July. The large, coarse, olive-green leaves are velvet-like to touch and contain

23

* Trimble Hot Springs reopened in 1988.

Hermosa House, the luxurious hotel at Trimble Hot Springs about 1900. Behind the hotel on the right were the bath houses and swimming pool. Many special trains carried excursionists from Durango, Silberton and other towns in the San Juans to this popular vacation spot.

(Collection of Kenneth Logan)

View southward of Hermosa, Colorado in about 1905 or 1906 by photographer W. R. Self. The buildings at the right of the track are a small depot, a bunk house and a section foreman's house. To the left of the track is a shed for tools and for a handcar. The siding at left probably has some of the original 30-pound rail, and the main line has at least a vestige of ballast.

(Center for Southwest Studies, Ft. Lewis College)

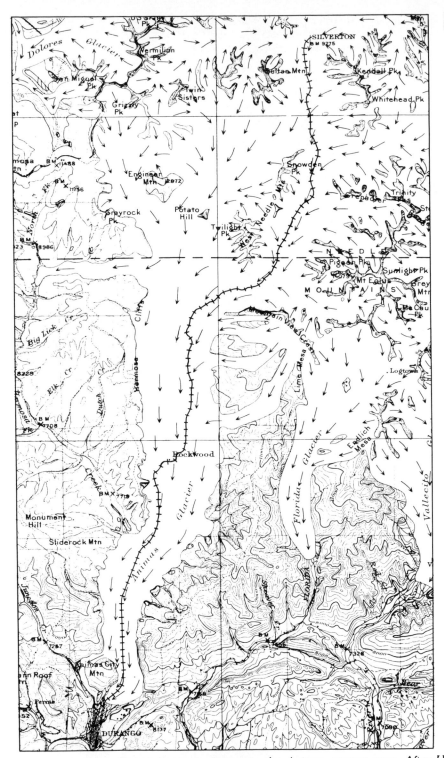

Maximum extent of the Wisconsin stage glaciers in the Animas canyon area. After U.S. Geological Survey, Professional Paper 166, plate 3.

chemicals used in lotions to soften the skin and in medicine to soothe inflamed tissues. Small birds eat the seeds in the dried, brown spikes when other food is covered with snow. The plant was brought to this country from Europe.

Milepost No. **CROSS HERMOSA CREEK.** The bridge is a 64-foot long wooden
462.4 pony Howe truss installed in 1914.

Milepost No. **HERMOSA.** Elevation 6645 feet. Water tank and passing track.
462.5 There was a wye and depot here years ago. Hermosa's first settlers
arrived in 1873-4 and in 1874 a post office was established. Mail
came via Howardsville, Silverton, and down the Animas canyon.
This was a regular stop on the toll road after it was established in 1876. A railroad construction camp was located here after construction started from Durango August 13, 1881; the track reached Hermosa in October, 1881. Ernest Ingersoll wrote an article about his experiences in this part of the Colorado Rockies in the April 1882 issue of Harper's Magazine.

" . . . Through the bottom we could see, running straight as an arrow, the graded bed of the coming railroad, but the stage-road kept away from it until we reached the few cabins that constitute Hermosa.

"Presently we came upon one of Mr. Wigglesworth's construction camps — long, low buildings of logs with dirt roofs, where grasses and sunflowers and purple asters make haste to sprout, are grouped without order. Perhaps there will also be an immense tent where the crew eats. Beside the larger houses, inhabited by the engineers, foremen, etc., you will see numbers of little huts about three logs high, roofed flatly with poles, brush, and mud, and having only a window-like hole to creep in and out through; or into a sidehill will be pushed small caves with a front wall of stones or mud and a bit of canvas for a door — in these kennels the laboring men find shelter."

This is the only description of a construction camp that was found during the research for this book. According to Mr. Robert W. Richardson, of the Colorado Railroad Museum at Golden, Colorado, few construction photographs exist of early-day mountain railroads in Colorado. He believes that the builders probably did not want prospective investors and stockholders to see the terrain and methods used to build these lines, because to Easterners the mountain construction must have seemed almost impossible. After a section of track was completed, then photographers were welcome to publicize the accomplishments.

Milepost No. **TRACK CROSSES U.S. 550.** The track gradually climbs (descends)
462.8 the side of the valley to by-pass the box canyon of the Animas
above Baker's Bridge. From milepost 462.8 to 464.2 the track wiggles along the slope in curves that range from 12° at 462.8 to 463.0
to as high as 24° at 463.8.

Milepost No. **GOOD VIEW EAST ACROSS THE VALLEY AND UP STEVENS**
463.0 **CREEK.** The brown, tan and gray cliffs are all part of the limestones, shales and sandstones of the Hermosa Group (labeled
Ph on maps) and vary from 630 to 680 feet in thickness. Good
photo spots of the flat valley floor are here. The train is beginning to climb into the timbered hills of the Transition Life Zone (see page 86). The trees along the track include Utah junipers with small purple berries, some quite large Gambel (scrub) oaks, and widely spaced ponderosa pines. Mullein and yucca are plentiful. The Indians made soap from yucca by pounding and pulverizing the roots.

In the spring of 1965, erection of a huge Yuba dredge in the valley was started to retrieve free gold believed to be mixed with the alluvial gravels and sands on the valley floor. This operation is now the site of a large concrete aggregate plant.

The beautiful rock work along the High Line is getting careful examination by the man in the foreground. Some of the original hand-hewn ties have been replaced by more modern sawed ties. The vertical black lines on the rock wall are 2½-inch steel rods, installed to insure stability; these were later replaced with old rails, some of which still remain. Even at this early date a guard rail was installed beside the inside running rail. This interesting photo may have been taken by Frank Gonner, an early-day Durango photographer. (Durango Public Library)

Monte Ballough took this beautiful photo showing the High Line above the Animas River and a large curved trestle at M.P. 470.2 in the right center. This photo was taken in 1903 or 1904 shortly before the trestle burned and was replaced with a fill. Grand View Park, on the slopes above the trestle, was a popular picnic spot for excursionists who took special trains to Rockwood for the day. The section men at the left are on a hand car that was propelled manually by pumping handles at each end up and down.

(Collection of Margaret Ballough Palmer)

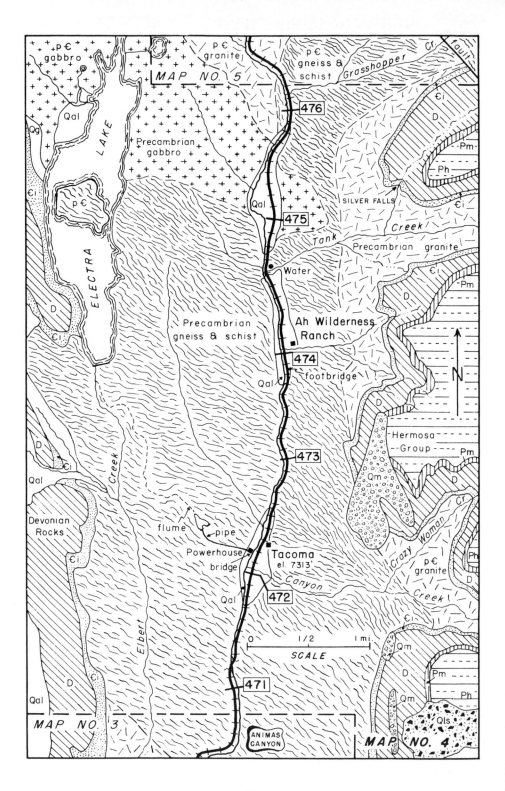

MAP NO. 5

p€ gabbro

Qal

Qg

p€

ELECTRA LAKE

Precambrian gabbro

p€

€i

D

€i

p€ granite

476

Qal

475

Water

Precambrian gneiss & schist

474

Qal

footbridge

473

flume

pipe

Powerhouse bridge

Qal

472

Devonian Rocks

€i

D

€i

Qal

D

€i

Qal

471

MAP NO. 3

ANIMAS CANYON

p€ gneiss & schist

Grasshopper Cr

fault

€i

D

Pm

Ph

€i

SILVER FALLS

Tank

Creek

Precambrian granite

€i

Pm

D

€i

D

Hermosa Group

Pm

Qm

D

Cr

Crazy Woman

p€ granite

Creek

Ph

D

€i

Qm

Tacoma el. 7313'

Canyon

SCALE
0   1/2   1 mi.

N

Qm

D

Pm

Ph

Qm

Qls

MAP NO. 4

Milepost No. 469.54 SAN JUAN NATIONAL FOREST SIGNPOST. Beside the track is an automatic wheel-flange oiler installed in 1981.

Milepost No. 469.6 ENTER (LEAVE) ANIMAS CANYON. SIGNPOST. Have cameras ready for the spectacular views as the train snakes along the High Line, the narrow shelf blasted out of red granite. The engineer has a permanent "slow order" through this gorge for the benefit of photographers and for safety. The water is more than 400 feet below the track! Wheel flanges squeak and groan, adding sound effects that will be hard to forget.

Milepost No. 470.0 UPPER END OF "SHELF" TRACK. At track level is the Central Claim, located in 1882, which contained a little gold and silver in a hematite-chalcopyrite quartz vein in faults. These faults are along the contact between the red granite and the older metamorphosed gneisses (pronounced, **nice**) and schists. In the fall, tall tansy asters and goldenrod are abundant along the track. There are many tall ponderosa pine and junipers.

Milepost No. 471.2 BRIDGE ACROSS THE ANIMAS RIVER. The bridge is a wrought-iron deck-truss bridge 130 feet long, built in 1880 and placed here in 1894. It was strengthened in 1981.

Milepost No. 471.45 SITE OF THE TRAIN WRECK shown in photographs on page 36. The river has cut down into the granite at places of least resistance (mostly along joints and fractures in the rock) to form a narrow post-glacial gorge. Highly metamorphosed gneisses and schists, which were formed from older igneous or sedimentary rocks by extreme heat and pressure probably as much as 2.5 billion years ago, are cut by white quartz veins. Some large masses of black hornblende gneiss and amphibolite (see Glossary, page 81) are found in ledges beside the track. Scrub oak is still very abundant, but firs are beginning to be seen and river willows are common. A spur known as SAVAGE formerly was at M.P. 471.7. Where the train passes close to the rock walls, notice the different colored lichens on the rocks. Lichens are primitive plants composed of food-producing algae and supporting fungi. They aid in decomposing rocks and producing soils. Their chief uses are in dyestuffs, antibiotics and model railroad scenery.

Milepost No. 472.05 TRACK CROSSES CANYON CREEK. CRAZY WOMAN CREEK SIGNPOST actually applies to a tributary of Canyon Creek (see Map No. 4).

Milepost No. 472.28 TACOMA. Elevation 7313 feet. Across the river is the Colorado-Ute Electric Association's Tacoma power plant, which was completed in 1905. Water to generate electricity comes from Electra Lake, a reservoir on Elbert Creek, about 1071 feet higher than the power plant. The water comes down the mountain-side by flume to a smaller reservoir and then into a penstock to the generators. A spur track to the power plant was washed out in the flood of October 5, 1911, when heavy rains widened the river channel at Tacoma from 90 feet to 170 feet. Twenty-two miles of track were destroyed in this flood. See photos page 38 and page 39. The alluvium (Qal on map) deposits which are mainly gravels and boulders deposited by the river, (shown on Map No. 4) contain glacial moraines at several places, and elsewhere consist of material reworked from former moraines. Retaining walls were built in 1970.

Milepost No. 473.0 ROCKS ALONG THE TRACK are dark colored gneiss with many small black inclusions (see Glossary, page 82) of older rocks and

On December 21, 1919 this mixed train traveling to Durango hit a rock slide south of Tacoma. The head engine, 270, jumped the track, took the flanger and engine 263 with it into the water. Fireman Hindelang jumped from the train and was not hurt, but Engineer Louis Johnson was injured and Fireman John Connor was crushed to death beneath the wreckage. Both engines were repaired and remained in service for many years. These two photographs were taken by Monte Ballough, a very capable photographer who was in charge of the D&RG wreck train at Durango. (Colorado Historical Society)

several white quartz veins. Between mileposts 473 and 474, the outcrops are of dark gray layered gneiss with intruded masses of diabase and some dark gray granite. White quartz veins follow the foliation. A dark reddish brown granite crops out on the cliffs above the valley. Although Map No. 4 shows the rocks between mileposts 471 and 476 as Precambrian gneiss and schist, other less abundant types are present, but are not shown to simplify the maps.

Milepost No. **474.0** **AH WILDERNESS RANCH.** Elevation 7473 feet. Only access to this guest ranch is by train, foot, or horseback. In 1981 the D&SNG bought 3 stock cars to haul horses to and from this ranch. The ranch is in a rather flat, U-shaped valley or park, that resulted when the Animas Glacier gouged out a long, narrow trough which was later partly filled with stream deposits of rounded rocks, boulders, and gravel. In the late summer and fall, when the level of the river is low, round holes or depressions in the rocks of the stream channel, called "potholes" are visible. The holes are formed by the grinding action of stones or gravel whirled around in one spot by the water. Wildflowers grow abundantly here. Only a few scrub oak grow at this elevation but aspen trees are becoming common. The aspen has a gray-green to white bark, and round green leaves that are nearly always moving, which gives it the name "quaking aspen" or "quakie." These slender, graceful trees often grow to 80 feet tall and may have a trunk 10 to 12 inches in diameter. From Ah Wilderness Ranch, looking out the east side of the train and to the north, **SILVER FALLS** shimmers in the sun as the water tumbles off a cliff of the Ignacio Quartzite (see map No. 4).

Milepost No. **474.65** **CROSS TANK CREEK. TANK CREEK TANK.** Footbridge. This roaring mountain stream heads on the southern slopes of Mountain View Crest. (See map on page 26). Northbound trains stop here to take water. This stop affords a good opportunity to see how the river has cut down through the gneiss and schist along joints and fractures. Track crosses another moraine. Water birch grows along the river and at the mouth of Tank Creek. This slender-stemmed tree with a shiny, dark bronze to copper colored bark grows to about 25 feet tall.

Milepost No. **475.0** **TALL TIMBER RESORT.** This resort is accessible only by train or by a big, self-propelled crew car from Rockwood. This open valley and aspen grove is a likely spot for wildflowers. The Colorado state flower, the blue columbine, thrives in moist, shady aspen groves. The beautiful blue and white spurred blossoms are 1 inch to 3 inches across and stand on slender stalks up to 2 feet tall. The columbine is found at elevations between 6,000 feet and 11,000 feet and blooms from late June in the lower elevations till mid-August higher in the mountains.

Although the track is on Quaternary deposits, Precambrian gabbro crops out on both sides of the valley between mileposts 475 and 475.6. This is a dark colored, medium to coarse-grained rock that was inserted as a hot fluid into the older gneisses and schists, probably about 2 billion years ago. Boundaries between the different types of igneous rocks are commonly irregular and indefinite.

Several movies have been filmed in this small park. A replica of an 1880 town was built near here for use in the movie "The Denver and Rio Grande." Parts of "Night Passage," "Ticket to Tomahawk," (see photos page 124) "Naked Spur," and "Around the World in 80 Days" were also filmed here, as were portions of "Butch Cassidy and the Sundance Kid."

Results of the October 5, 1911 flood at Tacoma. A spur track and bridge to the power plant were washed away and the river channel was 170 feet wide, instead of its normal 90 feet.
(Colorado Historical Society)

The destructive force of water is well illustrated in this photo of a rail that was driven through a firm river willow stump, as a result of the 1911 flood that washed away 22 miles of track.
(Colorado Historical Society)

As **The Silverton**, *pulled by engine 481, crosses the high bridge below Tacoma, the blow-off cocks are opened to force mud and other trash from the boiler.*

(Kenneth T. Gustafson)

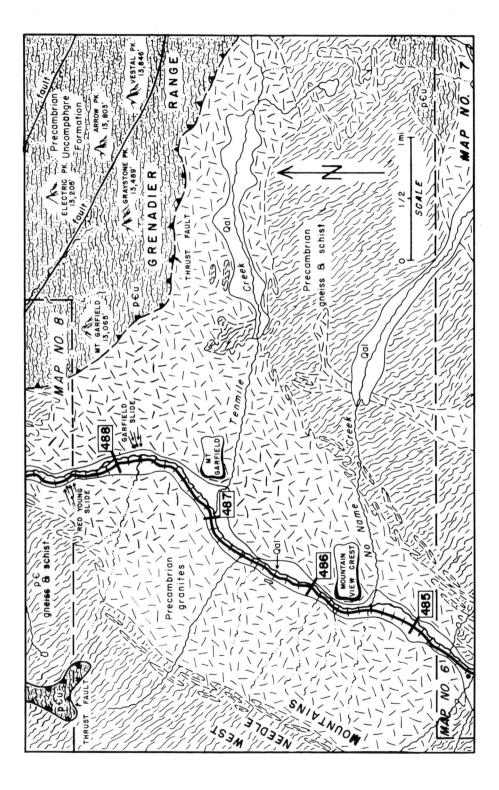

Milepost No.
484.5 **MT. GARFIELD AND MT. GRAYSTONE** of the Grenadier Range are now visible up the valley to the northeast. (See Map No. 7). Trees include alpine fir, willow, aspen, Englemann spruce and limber pine. The Englemann spruce is a compact tree up to 120 feet tall with a thick trunk. The bark is reddish-brown and thin with small loose scales. The needles are dark blue-green color, square and about 1 inch long. Needles of the firs are flat and blunt, while needles of the spruces are sharp and square, and needles of the pines are crescent-shaped. The limber pine is named for its flexible branches with needles about 3 inches long that are crowded in bundles of five at the ends of twigs. This conifer is from 25 to 60 feet tall. From here to Silverton the plant and animal community is typical of the Canadian Life Zone.

Milepost No.
484.6 **RUBY CREEK TUMBLES INTO THE ANIMAS CANYON.** Snowslide tracks and rock glaciers are along the west side of the railroad.

Milepost No.
485.0 **THE LIGHT GRAY COLORED GRANITE CLIFFS** here were rounded and smoothed by the Animas glacier.

Milepost No.
485.4 **NO NAME CREEK CASCADES THROUGH A MORAINE** into the Animas River. Rock slides and rock glaciers enter the canyon.

Milepost No.
485.7 **MOUNTAIN VIEW CREST SIGNPOST.** Good view south of this range. More potholes in the granite in the river channel are visible when the water level is low. Beavers have cut many aspen trees here.

Milepost No.
486.0 **GOOD VIEW OF HIGH PEAKS TO NORTHEAST.** A small stream enters the Animas from the east. Granite outcrops are rounded.

Milepost No.
487.0 **TENMILE CREEK TUMBLES INTO THE ANIMAS FROM THE EAST.** The old stage road is visible in the trees above the track. The mountain to the southeast is the westernmost extension of a ridge west of Monitor Peak. (See Map No. 6). A fan of stream alluvium and glacial debris has been deposited at the mouth of this valley.

Milepost No.
487.8 **GARFIELD SLIDE ACROSS RIVER.** Most years this large slide crosses the river and covers the track. This is one of the worst slides in the canyon. From here to milepost 495 the train crosses many snowslide tracks and landslides. The most difficult section of the track to operate is between here and Silverton because of snowslides, avalanches, and heavy rains. Every spring the line is opened by engines equipped with pilot plows and bulldozers hauled in to the slide areas on flatcars. So many rocks and logs normally are mixed with the snow in slides that rotary plows cannot be used.

Milepost No.
488.0 **ACROSS THE RIVER ARE THE REMNANTS** of a building used in a placer mining operation that was never successful because of the poor sorting of the stream gravel.

Milepost No.
488.5 **RED YOUNG SLIDE IS ON WEST SIDE OF THE TRACK.** It was named for an early-day engineer, William (Red) Young, who was killed when his engine slammed into a snowslide here in 1897. This is one of the few railroad fatalities that have resulted from a snowslide. Sometimes when the slides were particularly deep, it was easier to tunnel through them than to remove all the snow from the track. (See photo, page 119).

The southern slide off Garfield Peak at milepost 487.8 as it looked June 4, 1965.
(F. W. Osterwald)

This magnificent view of Electric, Arrow and Vestal Peaks, from right to left was taken August 11, 1903 by Ernest Howe, a U.S. Geological Survey geologist. He was across Elk Creek on a high ridge looking south or southwest toward the peaks. *(U.S. Geological Survey)*

First mixed train going through the Garfield Slide in February 1943 after it was cleared. That year the slide was from 4 feet to 75 feet deep and about 500 feet long. Combination car 212 is ahead of the caboose. *(Colorado Historical Society)*

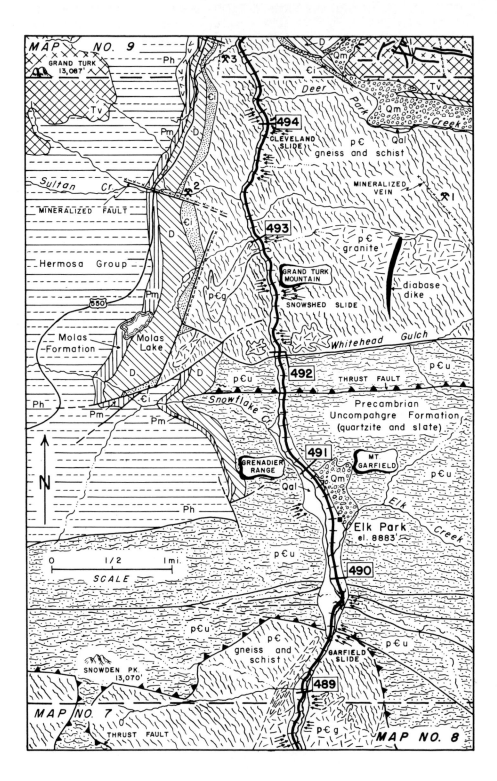

Milepost No. **489.0** **AN UNNAMED STREAM THAT HEADS** on the southern slope of Snowden Peak enters the Animas from the west. Snowden Peak is named for Francis M. Snowden, a miner who built the first cabin in Silverton.

Between Snowden Peak (Map No. 8) and Garfield Peak (Map No. 7) the Animas Canyon is 4250 feet deep and a little less than three miles wide.

The boundary between Precambrian granite and Precambrian gneiss and schist is very irregular and indistinct. The layers of the gneiss and schist stand vertically and make blocky cliffs. They are not rounded and smoothed as are the granite outcrops.

Milepost No. **489.55** **TRACK CROSSES THE SOUTHERNMOST FAULT** of the Grenadier Range fault belt. Here the Precambrian Uncompahgre Quartzite is faulted against Precambrian gneisses and schists. Note the tight folds in the shiny, gray quartzite which was deposited as sand by rivers flowing into a sea about 1 billion years ago. Between here and milepost 492 are several east-west trending faults (see Map No. 8).

The narrow V-shaped fault valley is the location of the second **GARFIELD SLIDE** that comes down the north slope of the peak. Snow still covers the river in early June in most years.

Milepost No. **489.9** **TRACK CROSSES ANIMAS RIVER** on a new 2-span, 222-foot deck plate girder bridge that was completed in 1964. The track makes a wide curve here before entering (leaving) the main part of Elk Park.

Milepost No. **490.0** **MILEPOST JUST NORTH OF OLD BRIDGE** on old section of track. (See Photo, page 125).

Milepost No. **490.2** **TRACK CROSSES ELK CREEK.** Folds in the Uncompahgre Quartzite are clearly visible to the west across the river.

Milepost No. **490.5** **ELK PARK.** Elevation 8883 feet. Siding and wye. In 1884 a stub switch with a harp-type switch stand was installed east of the track to turn trains after the track from Elk Park to Silverton was blocked by snowslides. The switch stand was removed by 1973. A large slide area is directly across the river.

A large moraine (Qm on Map No. 8) is along the east side of the valley. The river has reworked and shifted the morainal deposits, and combined them with stream gravel.

This open, grassy park is filled with many kinds of wildflowers. In the spring, white candytuft is common along with dandelions. Dandelions, which are socially unacceptable in lawns, are beautiful in the mountains in early June. The flowers and leaves are a favorite food of grouse, elk, deer, bear and porcupine. The roots have been used for centuries for tonics, diuretics, and mild laxatives. Summer brings the mountain parsley, ferns, columbines, Indian paintbrushes, shrub cinquefoil, penstemons, lupines, primroses and gentians. In September yarrow, goldenrod, fall asters and daisies are abundant.

To the northwest, Sultan Mountain is barely visible. On the return trip, look southward down the valley for glimpses of Graystone and Electric Peaks, along with a very good view of Garfield Peak. To the south, momentary glimpses of Arrow and Vestal Peaks will be seen before the train leaves Elk Park. See Map No. 7 for location of these high peaks of the Grenadier Range that stood above the surrounding ice during the glacial stages.

This photo was taken by Ernest Howe on August 11, 1903, one mile above Elk Creek looking south-southeast to Garfield Peak in the center and Electric Peak to the left.
(U.S. Geological Survey)

490.8 MT. GARFIELD SIGNPOST.

Milepost No. **491.0** NORTHERN END OF ELK PARK. The rocks in the stream channel are stained a reddish brown color due to chemicals in the water leached from the mill tailings ponds near Silverton.

Milepost No. **491.2** GRENADIER RANGE SIGNPOST. There are many good photo spots of the high country to the southeast. Tightly folded Uncompahgre Quartzite is visible here. The geologic structures along this section of the canyon are extremely complex, because the quartzite has been subjected to many periods of metamorphism and diastrophism, with faulting and folding. These structures are good examples of our wrinkled old earth.

Milepost No. **491.3** SNOWFLAKE CREEK, which heads on Molas Pass, joins the Animas here.

491.65 TRACK CROSSES A LARGE EAST-WEST THRUST FAULT.

Milepost No. **492.0** WHITEHEAD GULCH. The east-west fault that Whitehead Gulch follows is best seen looking west across the river. The fault brings the Uncompahgre Quartzite in contact with gneiss and schist. There are also two small, irregular masses (stocks) of reddish-pink granite that crop out on each side of the river. (See Map No. 8). The old toll road is visible on the hillside to the west across the river. Old rails still visible in the stream channel are the result of one of the violent floods in past years.

Milepost No. **492.5** SNOWSHED SLIDE. Timber sills and concrete walls remain from a shed 339 feet long that was built in 1890 to protect the track from two slides that come together at this point. The shed was burned July 23, 1917 and was replaced by a 400-foot long shed. From here to milepost 495 there are many slides, most of which have no name because they are too small or because they do not commonly cover the track.

Milepost No. **492.8** GRAND TURK MOUNTAIN SIGNPOST. The twin summits are visible to the northwest. See photo page 58, and Map No. 8. This is a good photo spot.

Milepost No. **493.0** IN LEDGES EAST OF THE TRACK are irregular tongues of a small granite stock that intrudes the older gneisses and schists. There is a good view of the Grenadier Range high country. Watch for likely photo spots on the return trip.

Milepost No. **493.35** SULTAN CREEK ENTERS THE ANIMAS FROM THE WEST. Molas Mine (No. 2 on Map No. 8) is in a mineralized fault, 1200 feet above the river. The Ignacio Quartzite, Elbert Formation and Ouray Limestone on the upper slopes to the west are near highway U.S. 550. Mine No. 1 shown along a mineralized vein due east of milepost 493 is the Mabel Mine; No. 3 is the King Mine.

493.6 TWIN SISTERS SLIDE.

494.0 CLEVELAND SLIDE. This slide runs regularly each year.

Milepost No. **494.2** TRACK CROSSES DEER PARK CREEK. Silverton water tank was located just south of the creek; it was demolished before 1924.

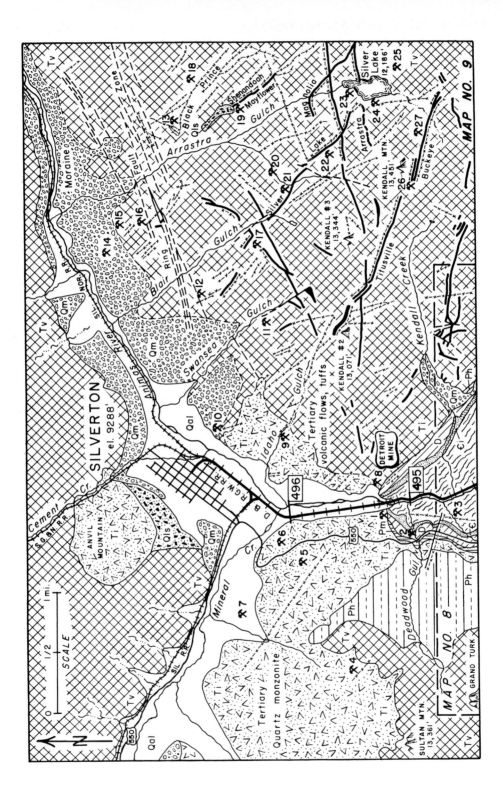

Milepost No. 494.55 **TRACK CROSSES KENDALL CREEK.** This gulch, which heads on Kendall Mountain, was named for L. B. Kendall, one of the original owners of the North Star mine.

Milepost No. 494.65 **CATARACT GULCH ON THE WEST.** The name is obvious in early June when snow runoff is the greatest. An aerial tram extended to the King Mine (No. 3 on Map on the west side of the canyon) from which silver and copper were produced. A spur track was located at 494.79.

Milepost No. 494.9 **LEAVE (ENTER) THE NARROWEST PART** of the upper Animas canyon. In the rush to finish the Silverton Branch, considerable trouble and delay was caused by the narrow canyon. SEE HISTORICAL NOTES, page 67. Notice the outcrops of banded, highly contorted and folded Precambrian gneisses and schists on both sides of the track.

Milepost No. 495.0 **DEADWOOD GULCH,** just north of the milepost, enters the Animas from the west. The **DETROIT MINE** (No. 2 on Map No. 9) is high on the west slope; water from the creek flows under the old building. Silver, zinc and copper were produced from this mine. A spur track to the tram station, on the east side of the mainline, was removed in 1924.

Milepost No. 495.2 **DECK TIMBER BRIDGE ACROSS THE ANIMAS RIVER.** The Ignacio Quartzite and Elbert Formation, dipping upstream, go under the stream gravels at this point. Schist and gneiss are under the Ignacio and Elbert. Some placer mining was carried on from the gravels at one time.

Milepost No. 495.25 **CHAMPION MINE** (Mine No. 1 on Map No. 9) adit, dump, and ore bin are on the west side of the valley. A spur track to the ore bin was removed in 1924. The mine is located on the contact of a Tertiary quartz monzonite mass that was intruded as a fluid into the Ouray and Leadville Limestones about 10 million years ago. Copper sulfide and silver-bearing ores with some zinc were produced from the mine in considerable quantities. The quartz monzonite is a light tan to buff to brown colored, fine-grained rock. Other workings on the same vein, up the hill near the highway, account for the bright green copper-bearing minerals that are being deposited along the steep gulch from water that flows out the mine portal.

Names of old mines shown on Map No. 9:

1. Champion Mine	10. Mighty Monarch	19. Shenandoah-Dives Mine
2. Detroit Mine	11. Scranton City Mine	20. Unity Mine
3. King Mine	12. Blair Mountain Wine	21. Nevada Mine
4. Belcher (Sultan Mtn.)	13. Little Giant Mine	22. New York Mine
5. Montezuma Mine	14. Amy Tunnel	23. Silver Lake Mine
6. Empire Tunnel	15. Legal Tender Tunnel	24. Iowa Mine
7. North Star (Sultan Mtn.)	16. Aspen Group	25. Royal Tiger Mine
8. Marcella Mine	17. Happy Jack	26. Titusville Mine
9. Idaho Mine	18. Black Prince Mine	27. Buckeye Mine

For opening day, May 23, 1981, the D&SNG ran a double-headed 15-car train pulled by engines 476 and 473. Both engines were working in the Animas canyon just below Silverton. The flags and bunting on the front of the lead engine were part of the opening-day ceremonies in Durango. *(Becky Osterwald)*

Silverton, Colorado in 1910, looking southwest down Greene Street toward Sultan Mountain. The city hall, built in 1907, is on the left. Photo by George L. Beam, a D&RGW photographer. *(Denver Public Library, Western Collection)*

Milepost No. 496.1 **TRACK CROSSES MINERAL CREEK** on a 112-foot steel plate through-girder bridge built in 1907 for the Colorado Springs & Cripple Creek District RR and placed here in 1916. On the west side, just above the valley floor are remnants of the Hercules Mine and Melville Mill. At milepost 496 a spur track turned northwest to the mill. Silverton is on the flat valley floor of Baker's Park. Baker's Park was the dumping ground for glacial ice that moved downward from Mineral Creek, Cement Creek, the upper Animas River and the gulches on the north side of Kendall Peak. Map No. 9 shows the lateral moraines along the sides of the valley northeast of Silverton.

Milepost No. 496.35 **WYE.** The train will turn here for the return trip to Durango. From 1887 until 1926 the Silverton RR went up Mineral Creek from the tail of this wye, and over Red Mountain Pass to Ironton, except for the period 1903-1912 when the Silverton RR used a new track on Cement and 6th Streets to get to its terminal. Ahead of the engine is Silverton, a typical mining town with the surrounding hills pockmarked with mine dumps, pits, shaft houses, shacks, and winding trails.

Milepost No. 497.13 **SILVERTON.** Elevation 9288 feet. The name was changed from Baker's Park to Silverton because as one early miner put it so succinctly: "We may not have any gold, but we have silver by the ton!" Track turns onto 12th Street and stops at Blair Street. This improvement was made in 1963 so passengers did not have to walk from the depot to the main part of town. In 1964 a second parallel track was built to 12th and Blair Streets, so now for several hours each day during the busy summer months, two engines stand side by side with steam slowly hissing from the escape valves.

Following a western style welcome, lunch at one of the many cafes or at the hotel, a tour of Silverton's shops and streets, and a visit to the most interesting San Juan County Historical Society's museum in the old jail, four long and loud toots of the train whistle summon everyone back to the train.

As the train starts back toward Durango, there are good views of Sultan Mountain, elevation 13,361 feet to the southwest, and the twin summits of Grand Turk, elevation 13,087 feet, to the left of Sultan Mountain. North of Silverton is Anvil Mountain. Kendall Mountain, to the east and southeast of Silverton, is now the site of most of the mining activity in the district. Map No. 9 shows a very generalized geologic map of the district with some of the mines, dikes and veins. Most of the mineral deposits were formed within the last 10 million years. The peaks are all capped by the San Juan Tuff that is about 500 feet thick in the Silverton area, and which consists of debris blown from old volcanoes about 20 million years ago.

As the train passes the wye and turns down the canyon, there is an excellent view of Garfield Peak in the distance ahead of the train.

This photo of Grand Turk Mountain was taken by Whitman Cross, October 9, 1901 from the east side of the Animas River. The old wagon road to Molas Lake switches back and forth along the side of Sultan Mountain. (U.S. Geological Survey)

HISTORICAL NOTES

DURANGO

Durango's birth was the direct result of the Denver and Rio Grande Railway's decision to build their expanding railroad system into the silver-ribbed San Juan Mountains. Mountain communities got their start when mineral deposits were discovered, but no real growth was achieved until the railroads, most of them "slim-gauge", arrived to take the ore to market and to bring supplies and people to the mines. As early as 1879, locating engineers of the D&RG were mapping possible routes into the mining districts of the San Juans. An article in **The La Plata Miner** published in Silverton, April 5, 1879 stated:

> "The struggle for priority of railway possession of the San Juan has now actively begun, and the shrill whistle of the locomotive and rumbling of cars over rocky beds will soon be echoing from the sides of these mountains."

By October 25, 1879 another article in **The La Plata Miner** reported:

> "A D&RG surveying party is now working on locating the line for the railroad in Animas Canyon. Surveyors have to be let down with ropes over the walls of the canyon in order to get the level."

In December, 1879, the railroad purchased the Animas Canyon Toll Road from the Wrightman Brothers. The Wrightman company had been issued their charter in 1876 to bring coal and produce to Silverton from Animas City. By February 1880, it was reported in the press that grading the roadbed had been started north of Animas City. By September, 1880 the D&RG had 551 miles of track and about 4700 men were working on different extensions of the railroad. This was an impressive record for a railroad that was only nine years old!

Earliest exploration into the Durango area is credited to the Spanish, who explored the southern slopes of the San Juans, and named many places. Escalante's diary for August 9, 1776 says, "We left the Rio Animas (River of Souls) and climbed the western slope." His expedition was seeking a route from Santa Fe to the California missions. Preceding Escalante, Juan Maria Rivera led several expeditions into southwestern Colorado between 1761 and 1775 looking for gold and silver. No diary of Rivera has ever been found, but some of the men who were with Rivera probably accompanied Escalante later, and pointed out previously named rivers and mountains.

The Animas River has been called **Rio de las Animas, Rio las Animas, Las Animas**, and **Rio de las Animas de Perdidas** in the literature and on old maps. **Perdidas** (purgatory in Spanish) probably was added to give a more romantic and descriptive name to the deep gorge of the river. This, however, has led to much confusion with the Purgatory River in eastern Colorado. Today the correct name is simply Animas River.

The next recorded explorer into the San Juans was Charles Baker, who led a group of miners up the Rio Grande, over Stony Pass, down Cunningham Gulch into Baker's Park, in 1860 or 1861. Winter found the group harassed by Indians, without much food or supplies; the survivors struggled down the Animas River to what is now known as Baker's Bridge (location is shown on Guide Map No. 3). Here the group spent the rest of the winter and left the area without finding much placer gold. Other prospectors wandered into the area; some names are recorded, others are lost to history. In 1868 the U.S. Government gave the Ute Indians title to the San Juan Mountains. Indian troubles multiplied with the increase in the number of prospectors, and by 1874 the government was forced to buy three million acres of mineral land from the Utes to pacify the Indians and to protect the miners. The purchase was called the Brunot Treaty and was signed in April, 1874. The last real Indian scare in the Animas valley occurred after the Meeker Massacre in northwestern Colorado, September 29 1879. Ft. Lewis was established at Pagosa Springs in 1872, but in October 1879 about 600 troops from Ft. Lewis, under the command of General Edward Hatch, marched to Animas City where a sod fort had been built, called Ft. Flagler. There were no skirmishes with the Indians as a result of the Meeker Massacre, but the troops helped calm both the settlers and the Indians. Troops remained at Ft. Flagler until January 1880 when they were transferred to Santa Fe, New Mexico.

La Plata County was organized in 1874 and Parrot City, (named for Tiburcio Parrot) became the county seat in 1875. Until the railroad arrived in Durango, Parrot City, located 12 miles west of Animas City, had a population of about 500 people, 3 grocery stores, 2 meat markets, 4 saloons, a post office, a courthouse and a jail. On August 30, 1880, Ft. Lewis was moved to a location two miles due south of Parrot City and remained an active fort until closed on October 15, 1891. The fort then became a school for Ute and Navajo Indians.

Animas City was the first town in the lower Animas valley to be established. The town site was surveyed in September 1876 and incorporated as a city, December 24, 1878. The town's first newspaper was **The Southwest.** Perhaps the paper's most famous quotation concerned the location of the new town of Durango, as proposed by the D&RG. The editor quipped May 1, 1880:

> "The Bank of San Juan has issued a circular in which it is stated that a branch office will be opened at the 'new town of Durango on the Rio Animas.' Where the new town of Durango is to be, or not to be, God and the D&RG Railroad only know. If they are in cahoots we ask for special dispensation."

Animas City lost and gradually business moved to Durango; on October 28, 1947 Animas City was annexed to the City of Durango. Railroad officials selected the name "Durango" from a similarly named Mexican town. It is hard to comprehend in this age of jet travel, how a town site (Durango), to which all supplies came great distances by pack trains, could be laid out in the spring of 1880 so that by September, lots were selling for $250.00 to $500.00, a brick yard and lumber yard were in business and a smelter was being built. **The La Plata Miner** reported on December 18, 1880 that many people were coming to Durango from Leadville. In fact, Durango's first newspaper press was brought by pack train from Leadville, and the paper was first published in a tent for an office. The owner, publisher, and editor was Mrs. C. W. Romney, a small good looking widow who put out the first issue of **The Durango Record** on December 29, 1880. On January 10, 1881, the newspaper moved into a "spacious" office and plant that was 22 feet by 50 feet in size. Her wit and sharp tongue make interesting reading.

The rapid pace of building and construction continued without interruption. By January 1881, the D&RG could boast owning 3000 freight cars, had purchased or contracted for 124 locomotives during the year past, had 684 miles of track, and steel rails were replacing the original iron rails. A large work force was constructing the grade between Durango and Silverton. By March there were 1000 people in Durango, 59 places where liquor could be obtained, and one church — the Episcopal church — which began to hold services in January. The town was eagerly awaiting the arrival of the railroad which was being extended over Cumbres Pass, criss-crossing the Colorado-New Mexico border before turning northwest toward Durango from Chama, New Mexico. The D&RG started in Denver in 1871, went south to Colorado Springs, Pueblo, and almost to Trinidad. The original charter was for a north-south railroad to El Paso, Texas via the Royal Gorge, across Poncha Pass into the San Luis Valley, and down the Rio Grande, by way of Santa Fe, Albuquerque and Mesilla. Seven branches were planned including one to Salt Lake City. The ores discovered in the Silverton region in 1872-4, caused the Rio Grande to pause in its southward journey and turn west toward the mining camps.

Every week the newspapers reported the number of miles the track was from Durango. On July 7, 1881, **The Durango Herald** had this headline:

"The railway is now within 18 miles of Durango and well informed persons express confidence that the track layers will reach this city before the close of the present month."

Construction continued at a feverish pace in spite of the trouble of keeping enough men on the work gang, delays in the arrival of ties and rails at the end of track, and of accidents. One accident about 20 miles east of Durango injured two men when a blast was set off prematurely. But on July 27, 1881 at 5 P.M. the first construction train arrived in the "city" of Durango, and the first passenger train steamed into town on August 1, 1881. The telegraph lines were completed on July 30. An interesting account of the arrival of that first train is given in volume I of the **San Juan Pioneers:**

"The track reached the corporate limits about 11 A.M. and when at 5 o'clock in the evening, the construction train reached G Street (9th Street now) in about the center of the city, the enthusiasm could no longer be restrained. Men, women, and children lined Railroad Street for nearly its whole length; sidewalks, doorways, and windows were crowded; the members of the City Band assembled at the corner of G and Railroad and commenced playing lively airs, and this of course brought out everybody.

Soon the officers of the City government appeared on the scene, in a body, headed by the Mayor with a silver spike and a hammer in hand — when all were assembled, our worthy townsman, J. L. Pennington, stepped forward, and with a claw bar extracted the iron spike inserted by the railroad men, then Mayor Taylor, spike mall in hand inserted a silver spike made from La Plata County ore, and with three terrific blows drove the spike clean in, thereby uniting Durango by a steel band, with the civilized world."

A grand railroad celebration was planned for August 5, 1881, but the August 5, 1881 **Durango Herald** reported:

"The unwelcome news was received in Durango this morning that the special train of Pullman cars, laden with gentlemen from Denver and other parts of the state, was detained at Navajo by a serious washout, and could not reach this city before night. This seriously interfered with the admirably arranged programs for our celebration today and was a source of unfeigned regret among all our people."

The program proceeded, however, without all the guests and dignitaries. There was a parade of the city police, city officials in carriages, and from Ft. Lewis came two companies of infantry, an artillary squad with gun, and the military band. The parade was followed by various races, a ball game, a shooting match and the day ended with a dance at the new smelter.

Mrs. Romney wrote of the first arrivals on the trains:

"The first freight delivered in Durango by the D&RG was an elegant omnibus for Myers and West. This large and handsome vehicle was placed upon the street on Tuesday and made a fine appearance. It is intended to carry passengers to and from the depot and hotels."

"The second train that came into Durango after the construction train, brought the pay car with paymaster C. A. Clark on board. First freight train came in on Sunday. It was laden with railway supplies. Since these first arrivals, trains have been coming in at all hours of the day and night, and no one would dream from the bustle and activity around the depots and the long trains of cars on the sidings, and the incessant movement of several switch engines that Durango had been other than an important railway center for years."

The above description gives a good idea of life in a railroad town. At this time, the Durango post office ranked third in the state, according to the number of business transactions, yet the town was three months less than one year old. In

Durango's San Juan smelter in about 1890. A stiff wind, blowing from the south, must have caused some air pollution in Durango!
(Durango Public Library)

View southwest of Durango in about 1910 toward the mouth of Lightner Creek. The smelter had been considerably enlarged and much of the vegetation on Smelter Mountain had died since the photo on page 62 was taken. The track of the RGS Railroad crosses the Animas River and extends up Lightner Creek in the right middle distance. Durango's prosperity was due largely to the smelter and to the railroads. Population was about 9000 at this time.

(Collection of Partridge Studio, Durango)

Rockwood, Colorado before 1891. These people probably were waiting for the stage to Rico. Notice the rough hewn ties placed directly on the ground, the light rail, and the false fronts on some of the buildings. The Hermosa Group of sediments form the towering cliffs on the skyline. The outcrop between the tall ponderosa pines is Ouray and Leadville Formations.

(Denver Public Library, Western History Department)

NEEDLETON

The old mining camp and stage stop of Needleton was located at milepost 482.31. This station on the railroad gradually grew more important as mining in the Needle Mountains, mainly up Needle Creek and the Chicago Basin area, started in the 1880's and early 1890's. Over $200,000.00 was produced from the district up to 1905. The **Durango Herald,** July 7, 1881 reported:

> "Reports from the Needle Mountains are most encouraging. A large number of assessments are being worked up there and some fine ore is being taken out. The camp unquestionably has a bright future when development begins in earnest and the extension of the D&RG road affords facilities for quickly transporting its ores to the smelter in Durango."

By 1883 the papers had reports of strikes and development work that were always described in the most glowing terms. For instance, **The Durango Daily Herald,** May 14, 1883 said:

> "We have just received trustworthy information that a series of the most wonderful strikes ever recorded in the state have been made in the hitherto almost unexplored region north, northwest, and northeast of Webb's great camp on the north slope of the Needles."

A sixth anniversary issue of the **Durango Herald,** December 24, 1887, reported that:

> "The mountains derive their name from the numerous needle and dome-like peaks that rise abruptly out of the surrounding mass of mountains, 10,000 to 12,000 feet in height. These needles and domes are set like mighty watch towers on the walls of the deep basins to guard the vast treasures hidden away in the great veins beneath. The views obtained from the summits of such of these towers as can be scaled by man, are vast and grand beyond description.
>
> ". . . The principal stream on the west, known as Needle Creek, finds its way in foam and cascade down through a wonderful canyon or crevice in the mountains to the Animas River, at Needleton Station of the Denver and Rio Grande Railway 30 miles north of Durango . . . A good trail or wagon road grade leads to the center of Chicago Basin, a distance of 6 miles."

By 1896 the post office, which opened in July 1882, was closed and the boom was over. The mineral deposits of the Needle Mountains district are very simple fissure veins filled with gold and silver bearing minerals and worthless rock. Most fissures are short, gradually pinch out into the country rock, and do not extend very far below the surface, because the upper parts have been eroded away. The veins are in metamorphic gneiss and schist and in granite. Most veins are in the granites, however, and have a high percentage of fluorite. The veins are low grade and were never very profitable to mine, but where oxidized the values are high. Unfortunately, oxidation was not very deep.

SILVERTON

In the rush to finish the Silverton Branch, much trouble and delay were caused because of the narrow canyon. It was difficult to get ties and rails to the end of the track. On June 1, 1882 the **Durango Herald** reported:

> "Five carloads of steel rails for the Silverton Extension arrived in Durango from Pueblo last night and were immediately forwarded to the front on a special train. The work of laying these rails was begun this morning and we are informed that the track layers will not again be delayed by a lack of steel."

Then on June 17, **The La Plata Miner** had a headline — "Tracks 13 miles from Silverton tonight." On June 27, the whistle of the D&RG work train was heard for the first time in Silverton. There were then 850 men working on the track which was 3½ miles from its destination. Grand plans were started to celebrate the arrival of the steel rails in "Silvery Silverton." Silverton was decorated with evergreen boughs, the 14-piece military band from Ft. Lewis was to play for the Firemen's Dance, and visitors from as far away as Denver were expected for the Fourth of July celebration. An article in the July 5, 1882 **Durango Herald** had a complete account of the events of the day. Several excerpts follow:

Silverton had a big year in 1879 because a good toll road was completed over Stony Pass. This cut down considerably the amount of time to get to the upper Rio Grande and on to Alamosa. Another sign of progress, in addition to the Melville Reduction Works, was a new brick plant that could produce 12,000 bricks a day. By 1883 the Grand Hotel was completed and opened for business and **The La Plata Miner** in the June 23, 1883 issue listed all the businesses in Silverton:

> "There are in Silverton 5 hotels, 10 restaurants, 34 saloons, 5 blacksmith shops, 8 laundries, 6 tobacco, fruit and candy stores, 4 livery stables, 2 bakeries, 1 theatre, 3 dance halls, 1 photograph gallery, 5 assay offices, 3 newspapers, 1 bank, 4 doctors, 2 dentists, 3 milling offices, 9 mining engineers, 18 lawyers, 294 dwellings, 2 hardware stores, 7 general stores, 2 clothing stores, 2 furniture stores, 2 harness shops, 4 meat markets, 3 drug stores, 3 jewelry stores, and 4 millinery and ladies stores."

An interesting description of Silverton in 1883 appeared in the **Durango Southwest:**

> ". . . As night darkens, the street scene changes from the work and traffic of the day and assumes quite a festive tone. Sweetly thrilling peals of music are borne upon the night air, and the brilliantly lighted, palacial saloons are thronged by the sportive element, with the pleasure seeking and curious, all classes mingling happily. The sharper with his trap-game laid for the sucker just fresh from the hills with too much dust or bullion certificates, or the greeny from the east with more of the Pop's bond coupons than he has of Ma's wit; either may be enticed by the glowing allurement."

The above quote gives a good idea of life in a growing, restless mining town in Colorado. Silverton was becoming very much a part of the "outside world" and it was possible to ride a through train from Silverton to Denver in 29 hours and 50 minutes. Residents probably felt that life was really becoming much easier. Then came the winter of 1884, perhaps the worst on record, and certainly one of the worst for the D&RG.

Snow started falling on Silverton and the surrounding mountains on February 2, and it continued for 20 long days. By February 9 there were 3 feet of snow on the ground in Silverton and drifts up to 7 feet deep. The railroad was blocked from February 4, to April 16 — 73 days all together. During this time numerous attempts were made to open the line. People in Silverton hiked 3 miles down the canyon to try and dig out the first slide, but there were two larger slides farther down the canyon that were too much for picks and shovels. One of these slides was 200 feet wide and 30 to 40 feet deep. A February 23, 1884 issue of **The La Plata Miner** fussed at the D&RG over this blockage; it suggested snowsheds and snowfences to protect the track. As if a fence could stop an avalanche of snow falling from one of the steep canyon walls. The article continued: "Our elevation is 3000 feet higher than Durango, but the railroad insists on bucking the drifts going up the grade." By March 1, a pack train arrived with needed supplies; it had come from milepost 492. Then on March 8, the newspaper was in a jovial mood when it wrote: "The D&RG RR though lost to sight, to memory dear . . . It is now thought that the D&RG will be extended to Silverton sometime in the spring. There are only 6 miles between here and Elk Park to be completed, and a large force — of wind is employed." By March the mines had to close down and the miners moved into Silverton. On Wednesday evening, April 16, 1884, the first train since February 3 arrived with two cars of merchandise, three cars of coal, two of grain and hay, and a small amount of fresh meat. The next day the train started back to Durango, but did not get through for another 24 hours. Other winters were severe and the line was closed by snowslides, but this was "The Winter" to remember.

By 1885, the population of Silverton had grown to approximately 2000 people, and Otto Mears' toll road over the "Rainbow Route" to Ouray was doing a brisk business. Often called the "Pathfinder of the San Juans", Mears decided in 1887 to build railroads instead of toll roads. He was the driving force behind the Silverton Railroad, a little line built to reach the rich mining camps of Chattanooga, Red Mountain and Ironton. The tracks reached Ironton in the fall of 1888 and the line did a thriving business until 1896 when the richest ores of the Yankee Girl and Guston were mined out and mines closed, partly as a result of the Silver Panic of 1893. The line limped along until 1926 when it was dismantled. Mears' next railroad venture was a proposed line from Silverton to Mineral Point, and possibly on to Lake City. The line, The Silverton Northern, was started from Silverton in April 1896 and reached Eureka in June of that year. It wasn't until the early 1900's that the line was extended to Animas Forks. The Silverton Northern continued in operation, sometimes intermittently, until 1942 when the company's three engines were sent to Alaska and the track was removed. The Silverton, Gladstone and Northerly Railroad was not started by Mears, but in 1913 he took over control of the company. The little line, all 7½ miles, ran up Cement Creek to the mining camp of Gladstone. Track laying started in April, 1899 and reached Gladstone by July. It was dismantled in 1938. Map No. 9 shows the location of these three lines.

Silverton had the distinction of being the only town in the United States served by four individual narrow gauge railroads. Three of these were headquartered in Silverton. Another honor for Silverton in 1962 was the National Park Service designation of the town as a National Historical Landmark. The bronze plaque from the Park Service is mounted on the wall of the old jail.

On June 1, 1967 the National Park Service returned to honor the Durango-Silverton narrow gauge D&RGW railroad. It was officially designated a Registered National Historical Landmark. In ceremonies in front of the Durango depot, Meredith Guillet, Supt. of Mesa Verde National Park, presented a certificate and bronze plaque to John Ayer Jr., Vice President of the D&RGW Railroad. This honor and memorial to mountain railroading is well deserved.

Another honor bestowed on the Silverton Branch was the designation as a National Historic Civil Engineering Landmark by the American Society of Civil Engineers in March, 1968. This award recognizes the tremendous part played by the civil engineering profession in surveying and constructing the branch through the difficult winter and spring of 1881-82.

FOR THE GEOLOGIST

SUMMARY OF THE GEOLOGY OF THE ANIMAS CANYON AREA

The San Juan Mountains probably contain as wide a variety of geologic structures, rocks, mineral resources, geomorphic features, and magnificent scenery as any mountain range in Colorado. From the oldest Precambrian rocks in the Animas canyon to the red, oxidized Tertiary volcanic rocks in peaks of the Silverton area, or to the beautiful glaciated horns of the Needle Mountains, the geology is doubly interesting because of the many geologic forms and the ease with which they can be seen. The following discussion summarizes briefly the major events of each period of geologic time and presents an idea of how the sequence of events was deduced. In general, old rocks are probably changed, altered, or metamorphosed more than young rocks. Thus events that happened during Precambrian time are extremely difficult to decipher, but events during the glacial stages can be deciphered from features observed in the valleys today. The San Juan Mountains are more than 120 miles from east to west and 90 miles from north to south, and are essentially a large, dissected dome that was repeatedly uplifted, eroded, and later glaciated.

PRECAMBRIAN HISTORY

Four major units of Precambrian rocks are in the Animas canyon. The oldest are ancient, highly metamorphosed gneisses, schists, granite gneisses, and amphibolites of unknown origin. These ancient rocks were folded, faulted, and subjected to extreme heat and pressure during several stages of mountain building. Later they were uplifted, and exposed to erosion. The second sequence of Precambrian rocks, the Needle Mountain quartzites and conglomerates, were laid down as sand and gravel by rivers upon a newly formed, submerged erosion surface cut on the old gneisses and schists. These Needle Mountain rocks were metamorphosed into hard quartzite now seen near Elk Park. During some time in the Precambrian, granitic rocks were injected into the gneisses and schists as a hot, fluid mass which gradually cooled into solid rock. These granites are classified according to their minerals into the Trimble, Eolus, Whitehead, Tenmile, and Twilight granites. These names have been omitted on the Guide Maps and all are shown as p Єg or p Єg granite. See the complete Geologic Column, page 76. The oldest Precambrian granites have been metamorphosed to granite gneisses. The gabbro which crops out near milepost 475 is a dark colored, medium- to coarse-grained igneous rock that was intruded into the old gneisses and schists.

PALEOZOIC HISTORY

At the end of Precambrian time the San Juan Mountains were eroded to a rather smooth, rolling plain that was gradually submerged beneath a shallow sea again. During Cambrian time the material that was brought into this sea by ancient rivers was deposited on the beveled surface of the Precambrian rocks as a thin layer of sandstone and conglomerate that is now hardened into the Ignacio Quartzite. Marine rocks were laid down beneath the sea during the Ordovician, Silurian, and Lower Devonian Periods, but all were removed, leaving only remnants of the Ignacio. Later the widespread marine Elbert Formation and Ouray Limestone were deposited above the Ignacio. A period of uplift followed the deposition of the marine Leadville Limestone, as shown by the sporadic distribution of the Leadville, and by its upper surface which is deeply weathered, and which contains sinkholes and caves filled with red muds that later hardened into the Molas Formation. During the Mississippian and Pennsylvanian periods, thick marine sediments (Hermosa Group) were deposited discontinuously for a long time in the San Juans, as shown by the types of rocks and fossils found in them. Conditions changed early in the Permian Period. Marine limestones and shallow water clastic sediments were no longer deposited, but streams flowing from distant mountains in an ancient desert, deposited red conglomerates, shales, sandstones and siltstones, termed the Rico, Cutler and the lower part of the Dolores Formations, some 2500 feet thick. The red shales probably formed as the clay and silt settled out on the flood plains of sluggish streams that may have drained to southeastern New Mexico and west Texas. The color of these "redbeds" is mainly iron hydroxide, which results from the rusting of iron-bearing minerals, mainly magnetite. The iron hydroxide forms a thin coating on the grains of sand and clay, and is mixed with the cement that holds the grains together. As a result, the rock is very intensely colored, but the coloring material makes up less than 1% of the rock. From 3300 to 4600 feet of sediments of Paleozoic age were deposited and gradually compacted and cemented into the rocks we find today.

MESOZOIC HISTORY

Mesozoic rocks are more than 8600 feet thick in the area between Durango and Silverton, and consist of alternating marine and non-marine types. The Dolores Formation, part of which is of upper Triassic age, represents a resumption of the "redbed" terrestrial deposition started during the Permian. Jurassic rocks consist of non-marine Entrada Formation, the Wanakah Formation, Junction Creek Sandstone and the Morrison Formation. All of these rocks are shown on the Geologic Column, page 76. The Entrada is a very distinctive, massive, cross-bedded white sandstone that was deposited in dunes that had little, if any, vegetation to hold the blowing sand. During the Cretaceous, great forests of deciduous trees, which were a source of food for the dinosaurs, grew in abundance, and were the source material for most of the thick coal deposits formed during this period. From time to time, ancient seas encroached upon the low land to deposit the marine shales, limestones, marls and sandstones. The coal beds near Durango formed in lagoons and swamps, and are either above or below these marine sandstones, depending on whether the sea was advancing or retreating from the land. Toward the end of the Cretaceous Period, the region was worn to a plain nearly at sea level. Near the end of the Cretaceous, the San Juan area was again uplifted and the previously deposited sedimentary and igneous rocks were eroded. Volcanic activity that culminated with the deposition of the rocks in the spectacular peaks around Silverton began near the end of the Cretaceous Period.

TERTIARY HISTORY

The modern San Juan Mountains were formed during the Tertiary and Quaternary Periods. At the start of the Tertiary Period, the Paleozoic and Mesozoic rocks were bent upward by regional doming so that they now slope away from the center of the dome, the Needle Mountains. The doming probably raised the mountains to at least 10,000 feet above the surrounding plains, and is the reason we see successively older and older rocks dipping beneath the surface as the train goes from Durango to Rockwood. This doming was followed by the emplacement of molten magma in dikes, sills and laccoliths during the Miocene and Oligocene Epochs. Afterward the San Juans were again eroded to a surface of low relief. The San Juan Tuff, which is 500 feet thick near Silverton, was deposited as rock debris blown from volcanoes during the

Era	Period	Symbols Used On Maps	Formation Name	Thickness In Feet	Description of Formation
CENOZOIC (Recent Life)	**QUATERNARY**	Qal			Alluvium. Loose rock deposits along stream channels.
		Qg			Pediments and terrace gravels.
		Qls			Landslides. Loose rock and soil from cliffs and slopes above slide.
		Qm			Moraines. Loose rock debris left by retreating glaciers.
	TERTIARY	Ti	Quártz monzonite stock; dikes of andesite, latite, granite porphyry, and rhyolite		Intrusive volcanic rocks — dikes, sills, batholiths, stocks.
		Tv	Pyroxene-quartz Latite	1000'	Extrusive volcanic rocks—flows, tuffs breccias.
			Burns quartz Latite	1200'	
			Eureka Rhyolite	1800'	
			San Juan Tuff	500'	Water-laid tuffs, agglomerates, small flows.
MESOZOIC (Middle Life)	**CRETACEOUS**		McDermott Formation	250-300'	These Upper Cretaceous formations do not appear on any of the guide maps.
			Kirkland Shale		
			Farmington Sandstone	1200'	
			Fruitland Formation	350-530'	
			Pictured Cliffs Sandstone	200-300'	
			Lewis Shale	1440-1825'	
		Kmv	Mesaverde Group Cliff House Sandstone	300-350'	Gray, marine, cliff-forming, calcareous sandstone that weathers to a rusty yellow-brown and red-brown color. Some sandy shale.
			Menefee Formation	125-630'	Gray and black shale and cross-bedded sandstone. Coal near top and bottom of formation.
			Point Lookout Sandstone	400'	Upper part is buff to white, massive sandstone. Lower part is thin, interbedded sandstones and shales.
		Km	Mancos Shale	1900-2200'	Dark gray to black, thin-bedded, marine shale with some limestone and calcareous shale layers.
		Kd	Dakota Sandstone	200'	Hard, brown, cliff-forming sandstones, with interbedded carbonaceous shale, conglomeratic sandstone and coal beds.
	JURASSIC		Morrison Formation Brushy Basin Member	500'	Greenish-gray to maroon bentonitic shale and mudstone interbedded with thin, greenish to gray sandstone beds.
			Salt Wash Member		Gray to brown sandstone with some interbedded red to gray shale.
		J	Junction Creek Sandstone	150'	Cliff-forming, white to buff, cross-bedded sandstone with some arkosic sandstone and shale.
			Wanakah Formation	50'	Made up of several members consisting of layers of reddish-gray sandstone, shale and marl. At the base, 2-3' of dark gray to black limestone (Pony Express).
			Entrada Formation	200'	White, cross-bedded, massive sandstone.

Note: The Tertiary latites, rhyolite, and tuff (Pyroxene-quartz Latite, Burns quartz Latite, Eureka Rhyolite, San Juan Tuff) are grouped as **Silverton Volcanic Series**.

Era	Period	Symbols Used On Maps	Formation Name	Thickness In Feet	Description of Formation
Mesozoic (Middle Life)	**UPPER TRIASSIC**		Dolores Formation	400-600' near Durango 40-100' near Ouray	Red, pink, purplish, and gray mudstone, siltstone, shale and sandstone with fossiliferous conglomerate near base.
PALEOZOIC (Ancient Life)	**PERMIAN**	"Redbeds" r	Cutler "Redbeds"	1900'	Dull to purplish red, coarse-grained arkosic sandstones and conglomerates interbedded with fine-grained limy shale, mudstones, and calcareous red shales.
			Rico Formation (or Basal Cutler)	100-165'	Red to gray-green to maroon, arkosic sandstone, limestone, and silty claystone.
	PENNSYLVANIAN		Hermosa Group Honaker Trail Formation	630-680'	Interbedded light gray and reddish arkosic sandstones, gray calcareous siltstones, and fossiliferous limestones.
		- - - Ph - - -	Paradox Formation	500-1300'	Dark gray to black shale, green to brown micaceous sandstone, some siltstone, evaporites, shale and limestone.
			Pinkerton Trail Formation	0-200'	Dark gray siliceous, fossiliferous limestone, and some interbedded gray silty shale.
		Pm	Molas Formation (locally present)	50-100'	Red calcareous, fossiliferous shale with limestone and chert nodules. Some sandstone and siltstone. Fills sinkholes in the Leadville Limestone.
	Lower Mississippian		Leadville Limestone (locally present)	100' at Rockwood; thins southward	Light gray fossiliferous limestone with chert nodules, oolite and some dolomite near base at Rockwood quarry.
	Upper Devonian	D	Ouray Limestone	70' at Rockwood quarry	White to buff to gray limestone and dolomite and some green shale partings.
			Elbert Formation	40-55'	Gray, green, red and purple shale; tan dolomite; red to white siliceous sandstone.
	Upper Cambrain	Є⊦	Ignacio Quartzite	70' at Baker's Bridge	White, pink, and red fine-grained, thin-bedded, quartzite or siliceous sandstone with conglomerate lenses and some sandy shale.
PROTEROZOIC (Before Life)	**PRECAMBRIAN**		Trimble Granite		Fine-grained gray biotite granite.
			Eolus Granite		Coarse, pink hornblende-biotite granite.
		p€g	Whitehead Granite		Reddish-pink biotite granite.
			Tenmile Granite		Pink and gray biotite granite.
			Twilight Granite		Light grayish-pink gneissic granite.
		p€u	Uncompahgre Formation	5500'	Massive, white or gray quartzite, locally congolmeratic with some dark slate and schist.
		+ + + + + + + + + + + +	Gabbro		Medium to very coarse grained intrusive rock that cuts the older gneisses and schists.
			Ancient granite gneiss, quartz-mica schist, amphibolite, gneiss		Finely foliated metamorphic rocks of unknown origin.

Miocene (?) Epoch. After this explosive vulcanism, deep gorges were cut into the San Juan Tuff. A complex series of lavas, tuffs and agglomerates known as the Silverton volcanic series, were deposited above the San Juan Tuff during the Miocene Epoch. These volcanics are thickest in a collapsed volcano north of Silverton known as the Silverton Caldera. This caldera is a basin about 8 to 10 miles wide that was dropped or faulted downward between 1000 and 2500 feet, at the same time that the Silverton Volcanic Series were being deposited in it. By late Pliocene time the San Juans may have once again been eroded to a surface of low to moderate relief.

QUATERNARY HISTORY

The transition from the Tertiary to Quaternary Periods was marked by further uplift, faulting and tilting of the mountain mass. Active erosion followed this uplift and produced a mature topography with deep canyons cut through the volcanic rocks sufficiently to expose older sedimentary and igneous rocks. Near the margins of the mountains the streams wandered laterally, cutting extensive erosion surfaces (pediments) that are mantled by thin gravels (Map No. 1). During this time the Pleistocene glacial episodes started. The glaciers of the first stage filled the higher valleys. As the early glaciers receded, further slight uplift caused the streams to renew their cutting; the San Juans as we see them today were beginning to take shape. Slight doming which occurred at this time may have resulted from a new magma moving into the area, but one that did not reach the surface. A second episode of glaciation filled the valleys and continued to scour and polish exposed rock surfaces. The last advance of glacial ice, termed the Late Wisconsin Stage, saw every major valley in the mountains filled with ice and the Animas Glacier, the largest glacier in the San Juans, reached as far south as the northern part of Durango (See Map page 26). This final glacial period left the summit peaks of the Needle Mountains and the Grenadier Range as tall, corroded, serrated horns, and the lower parts of the peaks, that were covered with ice, as smoothed and polished slopes. The peaks stood from 500 to 1000 feet above the snow fields. The terminal moraines left

Even after the arrival of the railroad in Silverton, this was the method of getting supplies to the mines in the high country and bringing the ore down to Silverton. The pack train is loaded with rails for use in a mine high above timberline. *(Colorado Historical Society)*

by this glacier are found in the low, rounded, hummocky hills near Animas City and elsewhere in the canyon, particularly where tributary streams join the Animas. After the last of the ice melted away, stream erosion continued to carve the valleys into their present form. The Animas River reworked and redeposited the glacial debris and cut a new, deeper channel down through the loose debris in many places. Elsewhere, the stream has followed the fractures in the granite and metamorphic rocks to carve deeper channels.

MINING IN THE SOUTH SILVERTON DISTRICT

The first successful mine in the district was the Little Giant in Arrastra Gulch in 1872, shown as Mine No. 13 on Map No. 9. Free gold was ground from the worthless rock in a primitive arrastra; the ore was placed in a circular stone bed, and heavy rocks were dragged around and around on top of the ore, usually by mules. In 1873 a stamp mill to replace the arrastra was installed about 1000 feet below the mine and ore was brought down on the first wire-rope tramway built in the region. Production from the Little Giant in 1873 was $12,000.00, but the main pay began to diminish. The big rush to the San Juans began in 1874 with silver strikes principally on Hazelton Mountain. The machinery to build the Greene and Co. Smelter was brought to Silverton by pack train from Colorado Springs in 1874. The drawing on page 70 shows the location of this smelter. The bullion from the smelter was shipped to Pueblo via pack train at $60.00 a ton. Before the arrival of the D&RG, ores worth less than $100.00 per ton could seldom be handled for a profit; after the railroad started to haul ore to the smelter in Durango, low grade ores could be handled profitably.

The Silver Lake mine became a good producer in 1883, as did the North Star on Sultan Mountain, Belcher, Aspen, Gray Eagle, North Star on Solomon Mountain and Green Mountain mines. Ores in which silver and lead are the main metals are produced from most of the mines. The Silver Panic of 1893 caused many mines to close, but the attempts to mine and concentrate the larger bodies of low-grade ores were continued. Today low-grade ores containing gold, silver, copper, lead and zinc are produced. D. J. Varnes estimated that total production of ore through 1957 was at least $61,000,000.00 and was probably greater. Rhodochrosite, a pink-colored manganese carbonate, is obtained from the Shenandoah-Dives mine. This mineral and other ore specimens are sold along the streets in Silverton by the local children.

The ore deposits of the South Silverton district occur in veins of a complex fracture zone that is south and southeast of the ring faults, which roughly mark the southern boundary of the Silverton Caldera. The ring fault zone, shown on Map No. 9, contains many veins, but most are not productive. The fractures that controlled ore deposition can be classified into three systems: 1) unmineralized concentric fractures and dikes that parallel the border of the subsided Silverton Caldera, 2) mineralized northwest shear fractures and north-northwest trending tension fractures, and 3) an eastern shear system of curving granite porphyry dikes. Map No. 9 shows, in a very generalized way, the mineralized faults and the andesite and/or latite dikes that vary from a few inches to broad zones 100 feet or more in width. Only a few of the hundreds of mines and prospects can be shown on a map of this scale. The principal mineralized dikes are also shown. The mines at or near the contact of Paleozoic rocks and volcanic rocks are replacement-type ore deposits, which means that certain constituents of the rock have been carried away in solution and other minerals, usually the ore-bearing minerals, have been deposited in their place.

79

W. H. Jackson, famous "Picture Maker of the West," took this photo of a prospector's camp high on the slopes of Cunningham Gulch, east of Silverton in 1875. Any suggestions as to the contents of the sacks on the right side of the photo?   (U.S. Geological Survey)

View northwest across Silver Lake, a cirque lake in a basin formed by glaciers (shown on Map No. 9). Elevation at the lake is 12,186 feet, and all supplies and equipment were brought up Arrastra Gulch (in background), to the Silver Lake mine, first by pack trains and later by wagons and trucks. David J. Varnes, a U.S. Geological Survey geologist, took this photo in 1946.   (U.S. Geological Survey)

GLOSSARY OF GEOLOGIC TERMS

Definitions are from Stokes, W. L. and Varnes, D. J., 1955, Glossary of Selected Geologic Terms: Colorado Scientific Society, Proceedings, vol. 16.

The following list is reproduced with the permission of and thanks to the Colorado Scientific Society.

agglomerate, n. A mass of unsorted volcanic fragments which may be loose or consolidated into a solid mass by finer volcanic material which fills the interstices.

alluvial fan, n. A sloping, fan-shaped mass of loose rock material deposited by a stream at the place where it emerges from an upland into a broad valley or a plain.

alluvium, n. A general term for all detrital material deposited permanently or in transit by streams. It includes gravel, sand, silt, clay, and all variations and mixtures of these.

alpine glacier, n. The type of glacier that forms in the valleys and about the higher peaks of mountains. Such glaciers originate in rather broad amphitheatres at higher elevations and usually become concentrated in valleys at lower elevations.

amphibolite, n. A rock in which the amphibole group of minerals predominate.

andesite, n. A common volcanic rock in which the soda-lime feldspars, generally oligoclase or andesine, predominate over the alkalic feldspars, and which contains one or more of the dark minerals, biotite, hornblende, diopside, augite, hypersthene, etc. Quartz, if present, is hidden in the ground-mass.

argillite, n. Argillite is defined as a rock derived either from siltstone, claystone, or shale, that has undergone a somewhat higher degree of induration than is present in those rocks. Argillite holds an intermediate position between the rocks named and slate. Cleavage is approximately parallel to bedding in which it differs from slate (Twenhofel, 1938).

basal conglomerate, n. A conglomerate that lies immediately above an unconformity and constitutes an initial or introductory phase of the overlaying beds. Typically, a basal conglomerate represents the accumulation of beach material laid down by an advancing ocean.

basalt, n. In the general usage, the term includes the majority of fine-grained, dark, heavy volcanic rocks. No strict definition of basalt as a mineralogic or chemical type is yet agreed upon, nor are there definite criteria for distinguishing some basalts from andesite.

batholith, n. A very large mass of intrusive rock, generally composed of granite or granodiorite, which, in most cases, cuts across the invaded rocks, and shows no direct evidence of having a floor of older solid rock.

boundary, n. A term used in connection with geologic mapping to designate the contact between different types or ages of rocks or other earth materials.

breccia, n. A rock consisting of consolidated angular rock fragments larger than sand grains. It is like conglomerate, except that most of the fragments are angular with sharp edges and unworn corners.

caldera, n. Calderas are large volcanic depressions, more or less circular or cirque-like in form, the diameters of which are many times greater than those of the included vent or vents, no matter what the steepness of the walls or form of the floor. With rare exceptions all volcanic depressions of the characters defined are caused primarily by collapse.

chalcopyrite, n. Yellow copper and iron sulfide ore mineral.

cirque, n. An amphitheatre-shaped depression formed in the higher parts of mountain ranges as a consequence of the disruption of rock by frost action around a snow field. The cirque hollow or recess is gradually enlarged as the broken rock is carried away by slowly moving snow and glacial ice (After Putnam).

clastic rocks, n. Include those deposits which are made up of fragments of pre-existing rocks, or of the solid products formed during the chemical weathering of such older rocks. Familiar examples of sediments belonging to this group are gravel, sand, mud, and clay, and their consolidated equivalents, conglon-e rate, sandstone, and shale.

columnar section, n. A geologic illustration that shows in a graphic manner, and by use of conventional symbols for different rock types, the successive rock units that occur throughout a given area or at a specific locality.

conglomerate, n. The consolidated equivalent of gravel. The constituent rock and mineral fragments may be of varied composition and of a wide size range. The rock fragments are rounded and smoothed from transportation by water, or from wave action.

contact, n. The surface, often irregular, which constitutes the junction of two bodies of rock different in kind, age, or origin (Merriam-Webster).

cycle of erosion, n. The complete series of changes or stages through which a land mass passes from the inception of erosion on a newly uplifted or exposed surface through its dissection into mountains and valleys to the final stage when it is worn down to the level of the sea or other base level. The cycle is usually subdivided into youthful, mature, and old-age stages.

diabase, n. A basic igneous rock of the basalt-gabbro series in which the essential minerals are plagioclase and augite with the plagioclase in long, narrow, lath-shaped crystals oriented in all directions and the augite filling the interstices.

diastrophism, n. The process or processes by which the earth's crust is deformed, producing continents and ocean basins, plateaus and mountains, folds of strata, and faults; also, the results of these processes (Merriam-Webster).

dike, n. A sheet-like body of igneous rock that fills a fissure in older rocks which it entered while in a molten condition. Dikes occur in all types of material, igneous, metamorphic, and sedimentary.

dolomite, n. A calcium-magnesium carbonate rock.

dome, n. (Structural Geology) An anticlinal uplift approximately circular or elliptical in plan.

epidote, n. A basic orthosilicate mineral of calcium and aluminum with variable iron. Epidote commonly occurs in rocks as formless grains and masses.

extrusive, 1. adj. Pertaining to igneous material poured out on the surface of the earth in a molten state and to fragmental material of all sizes erupted from volcanic vents. Lava flows and tuff beds are common examples. **2. n.** An extruded rock or body.

fault, n. A break in materials of the earth's crust on which there has been movement parallel with the surface along which the break occurs. A fault occurs when rocks are strained past the breaking point and yield along a crack or series of cracks so that corresponding points on the two sides are distinctly offset. One side may rise, or sink, or move laterally with respect to the other side.

fissure vein, n. A fissure vein is a tabular ore body that occupies one or more fissures; two of its dimensions are much greater than the third. Fissure veins are the most widespread and important of the cavity fillings and yield a great variety of minerals and metals.

flow, n. That which flows or results from flowage; as, for example, a lava flow.

fold, n. A bend or flexure in a layer or layers of rock.

foliation, n. The banding or lamination of metamorphic rocks as contrasted with the stratification of sediments. Foliation implies the ability to split along approximately parallel surfaces due to the parallel distribution of layers or lines of one or more conspicuous minerals in the rock. The layers may be smooth and flat or they may be undulating or strongly crumpled.

formation, n. The formation is the fundamental unit in the local classification of rocks. The larger units, groups and series, may be regarded as assemblages of formations and the smaller units as subdivisions of formations.

fracture, n. A crack in a rock large enough to be visible to the unaided eye. It may be a joint, fault, or fissure, but use of the term usually implies that the surfaces of the break are not in absolute contact.

gabbro, n. Dark, equigranular igneous rock which consists of calcic plagioclase, such as labradorite, or bytownite, and one or more dark minerals. The common dark minerals are hornblende, pyroxene, and olivine. Magnetite, ilmenite, and apatite are accessory minerals. Gabbro makes up vast bodies of rock. The extrusive equivalent is basalt.

glacier, n. A body of ice consisting of recrystallized snow, lying wholly or largely on land, and showing evidence of present or former flow. (Flint, 1947).

gneiss, n. A foliated metamorphic rock with no specific composition implied, but having layers that are mineralogically unlike and consisting of interlocking mineral particles that are mostly large enough to be visible to the eye. A somewhat arbitrary distinction between schist and gneiss is that based on the presence of feldspar in gneiss and its absence in schist. Various types are recognized; as, granite gneiss, quartzite gneiss, conglomerate gneiss, mica gneiss, hornblende gneiss, and gabbro gneiss.

granite, n. A true granite is a visibly granular, crystalline rock of predominantly interlocking texture, composed essentially of alkalic feldspars and quartz.

gravel, n. Loose or unconsolidated coarse granular material, larger than sand grains, resulting from erosion of rock by natural agencies.

hematite, n. One of the common ore minerals of iron, having the composition Fe_2O_3.

horn, n. A sharp pyramidal peak in a mountainous region. Typical horns are cut by the headward sapping of three or more glacial cirques.

igneous rocks, n. Rocks formed by solidification of hot mobile rock material (magma) including those formed and cooled at great depths (plutonic rocks), which are crystalline throughout, and those which have poured out on the earth's surface in liquid state or have been blown as fragments into the air (volcanic rocks). Igneous rocks comprise the bulk of the earth's crust. They occur in bodies with a variety of shapes such as flows, dikes, sills, and batholiths.

inclusion, n. A general term for any body of foreign material, gas, liquid, or solid, inclosed in a mineral or rock. Also by extension, any fragment of foreign material inclosed in any kind of rock.

interstice, n. An opening, void, or space between one thing and another. In geology, it is a space in rock or soil that is not occupied by solid mineral matter. It may be occupied by air, water, or other gaseous or liquid material.

intrusion, n. The process of forcible implacement of one body of mobile rock material into or between other rocks. The term generally refers to the invasion of older rocks at depth by molten rock or magma; but it is also used to describe the plastic injection of salt domes into overlying rocks.

joint, n. A fracture or parting plane along which there has been little if any movement parallel with the walls.

laccolith, n. An injected lens- or dome-shaped mass of igneous rock approximately concordant with the enclosing strata and having its roof so bulged as to produce a distinct anticline in the overlying strata.

lateral moraine, n. A ridge or belt of glacial material being transported by a glacier or deposited at its side. It is composed of debris that was acquired by abrasion and quarrying or that has fallen down upon the margins of the glacier from the confining walls of higher elevations.

latite, n. An extrusive igneous rock in which the feldspars, plagioclase and orthoclase, are present in about equal amounts, and free quartz is absent.

lava, n. A general name for molten rock poured out upon the surface of the earth by volcanoes and for the same material that has cooled and solidified as solid rock.

limestone, n. Strictly defined, limestone is a bedded sedimentary deposit consisting chiefly of calcium carbonate ($CaCO_3$) which yields lime when burned. Limestone is the most important and widely distributed of the carbonate rocks and is the consolidated equivalent of limy mud, calcareous sand, or shell fragments.

magma, n. Hot mobile rock material generated within the earth, from which igneous rock results by cooling and crystallization.

magnetite, n. A black native oxide of iron which is strongly attracted by a magnet: An important iron ore (Century Dictionary).

marl, n. An old term loosely applied to a variety of materials most of which occur in loose, earthy, or friable deposits and contain a relatively high proportion of calcium carbonate or dolomite.

metamorphism, n. The mineralogical and structural adjustment of solid rocks to physical or chemical conditions that have been imposed at depths below the surface zones of weathering and cementation, and which differ from the conditions under which the rocks in question originated (Turner).

monadnock, n. An isolated high point, which, because of greater resistance to erosion or some other cause, remains projecting above the general surface of an almost level plain.

monzonite, n. An igneous rock of granular, interlocking texture composed mainly of plagioclase and orthoclase feldspar and one or more dark minerals. The two types of feldspar occur in approximately equal amounts and the monzonites may be regarded as forming connecting links between the diorites and syenites. Quartz is typically absent; when it is present the rock is called quartz-monzonite.

moraine, n. An accumulation of drift with an initial topographic expression of its own, built within a glaciated region chiefly by the direct action of glacier ice (Flint). Many kinds have been named: dump, frontal, ground, lateral, medial, terminal, etc.

mudstone, n. Consolidated mud or clay that shows little or no tendency to break into thin layers like shale.

outcrop, n. A part of a body of rock that appears, bare and exposed, at the surface of the ground.

oxidation, n. In the process of oxidation, oxygen is added to the rocks, especially to the iron compounds. The oxidation of rocks by air is aided by the presence of moisture; without water, oxidation is generally slow.

oxidized zone, n. The part of an ore body in which surface waters carrying oxygen, carbon dioxide, etc., have been active. It is the zone in which sulfides have been altered to oxides and carbonates.

pediment, n. A gently inclined erosion surface of low relief typically developed in arid or semiarid regions at the foot of a receding mountain slope. The surface is usually underlain by rocks of the upland, and thus may cut across rocks of various compositions and structures. The pediment may be bare or mantled by a thin layer of alluvium which is in transit to the adjoining basin.

placer, n. A deposit of sand or gravel, usually of fluvial origin, containing particles of gold or other valuable mineral.

porphyry, n. An igneous rock containing a considerable proportion, say 25 percent or more by volume, of larger crystals, phenocrysts, set in a finer groundmass of small crystals or glass or both. The rock name applicable to the groundmass part of the rock is usually prefixed to the word porphyry (i.e granite porphyry).

pyrite, n. A common mineral having the composition FeS_2, a pale brass-yellow color, and brilliant metallic luster.

quartz, n. Anhydrous crystalline silica, SiO_2. Quartz is the most common of minerals and has widespread occurrence in igneous, sedimentary, and metamorphic rocks.

quartz monzonite, n. A rock of granitic texture, intermediate in composition between granite and quartz diorite, which contains quartz and about equal amounts of the alkali and soda-lime feldspars.

quartzite, n. A quartz rock derived from sandstone, composed dominantly of quartz, and characterized by such thorough induration, either through cementation with silica or through recrystallization, that it is essentially homogenous and breaks with vitreous surfaces that transect original grains and matrix or interstitial material with approximately equal ease.

rock glacier, n. An accumulation of broken rock fragments and finer-grained material that moves slowly but perceptibly downhill under its own weight and with the aid of interstitial ice. Rock glaciers usually occur in high mountains and somewhat resemble true ice glaciers in location, shape and movement.

sandstone, n. A consolidated rock composed of sand grains cemented together. Although sandstones may vary widely in composition they are usually made up of quartz.

schist, n. A crystalline metamorphic rock that has closely spaced foliation and tends to split into thin flakes or slabs. There is complete gradation between slates and schists on the one hand and schists and gneisses on the other. In general, however, schists show a coarser texture and a more evident crystallization than slates and they have a higher proportion of secondary minerals and a more regular and closely spaced lamination than gneisses.

sedimentary rock, n. Sedimentary rocks are those composed of sediment: mechanical, chemical, or organic. They are formed through the agency of water, wind, glacial ice, or organisms and are deposited at the surface of the earth at ordinary temperatures. The materials from which they are made must originally have come from the disintegration and decomposition of older rocks, chiefly igneous.

shale, n. A general term for lithified muds, clays, and silts that are fissile and break along planes, parallel to the original bedding. A typical shale is so fine-grained as to appear homogeneous to the unaided eye, is easily scratched and has a smooth feel.

sill, n. A tabular body of igneous rock that has been injected while molten between layers of sedimentary or igneous rocks or along the foliation planes of metamorphic rocks. Sills have relatively great lateral extent as compared with their thickness.

slate, n. A homogeneous, metamorphic rock, so fine-grained that no mineral grains can be seen. Most slates are blue-black, a shade so typical as to be called slate-colored, but many are red, green, gray, or black. Slate splits with a foliation so perfect that it yields slabs having plane surfaces almost as smooth as the cleavage planes of minerals.

stock, n. An irregular body of intrusive rock having a roughly conical or blunt cylindrical shape. It shows no evidence of having a floor.

The horizontal cross sections are relatively small, and in any case should not exceed the arbitrary limit of about 40 square miles which marks the lower size of batholiths. Stocks cut across the enclosing rocks and many have steeply dipping contacts, along which characteristic metamorphism or ore deposition has occurred.

terminal moraine, or end moraine, n. This is a ridgelike accumulation of drift built chiefly along the terminal margin of a valley glacier or the margin of an ice sheet. It has a surface form of its own and is the result chiefly of deposition by the ice, or deformation by ice thrust, or both. The essential thing about end moraine is its close relationship to the terminus or margin of the glacier.

travertine, n. The rock formed by deposition of calcium carbonate from solution is called travertine, from the old Roman name of the town of Tivoli near Rome, where an extensive formation of it exists.

tuff, n. Indurated pyroclastic material, consisting wholly or predominantly of fine-grained volcanic ash or dust.

vein, n. A mineral mass having well-defined length, width, and depth and clearly distinguishable in mineral content and structure from the enclosing rock.

volcanic rocks, n. Rocks that have issued from vents at the earth's surface, either ejected explosively (pyroclastic material) or extruded as lava, together with the near-surface dikes, sills and plugs which form a part of the volcanic structure. Such rocks because they solidify by rapid cooling from a high temperature and with some loss of volatile constituents, are generally finely crystalline or glassy.

On May 24, 1981, the second day of operations for the D&SNG, this double-header started the steep climb to Rockwood after passing Hermosa on its way to Silverton.
(F. W. Osterwald)

FOR THE NATURALIST

LIFE ZONES

Life zones are communities of plants and animals that have achieved a balance between climate, (which is related to latitude) and altitude. High latitude has the same effect on the growth of plants as does high altitude at a much lower latitude. Because of this fact, flowers that we find only above timberline in Colorado (11,500 feet) will be growing in southern Wyoming at about 10,500 feet, or 9,000 feet in Montana, and at sea level near the Arctic Circle. Thus it is possible to make this train trip in June and see purple fringe (phacelia) blooming along the tracks near Durango, but by mid-August, the same plant will be in full bloom in Silverton. Plant and animal zones are not sharp boundaries; they merge into each other. Many flowers are found in two or more zones. Growth is dependent upon moisture, soil, wind and slope conditions. Often one zone will be present on a north-facing slope, and a different zone or plant community will be found on the south-facing slope directly across the valley. The following table shows the life zones of Colorado and the most common trees, shrubs, flowers, animals and birds found in each zone. The trip to Silverton passes from the Transition Zone into the Canadian Zone. (See Diagram, page 87.)

ALPINE (ARCTIC) ZONE. Over 11,500 feet altitude. Corresponds to 66° N. Lat.

Trees: The climate is too severe for trees. Tundra and cushion-type plants with almost no stems are common, as are sedges, dwarf willows, shrubby cinquefoil, and bog birch.

Flowers: Flower blossoms are usually small and delicate. Melting snowbanks supply plenty of water for the flowers that begin to appear in the early summer. These include alpine phlox, sky pilot, moss campion, alpine avens, glacier lily, alpine forget-me-not, alpine lily, alpine columbine, alpine wallflower, candytuft, snow buttercup, globeflower, queen's crown, and king's crown. In late summer the arctic gentian, bistort, yellow paintbrush and yarrow appear.

Birds: White-tailed ptarmigan, rosy finch, water pipit, horned lark and white-crowned sparrow.

Mammals: Pika or coney, northern pocket gopher, mountain sheep, marmot, and hoary marmot.

HUDSONIAN (SUB-ALPINE) ZONE. 10,000 feet to 11,500 feet altitude. Corresponds to 60° to 66° N. Lat.

Trees: Englemann spruce, subalpine fir, limber pine and bristlecone pine. These forests are abundant in areas of heavy snow and frequent summer rains.

Flowers: In this zone are found a luxuriant growth of wildflowers in meadows, ponds and peat bogs. Flowers do well in this zone because of heavy winter snowfall that melts slowly and supplies plenty of water to the lush meadows and open forests. Late spring and early summer flowers include moss campion, monkshood, marsh marigold, alpine sunflower, alpine buttercup, globeflower, wallflower, rose crown, strawberries, kinnikinnick, shooting star, Parry's primrose, green gentian, sky pilot, white phlox, purple fringe, little red elephant, penstemons, glacier lily, and columbine. By summer and early fall the fringed gentian, tall chiming bell, harebell, yarrow, stonecrop, goldenrod, and composites are blooming at these elevations.

Birds: Canada jay (camp robber), Audubon's hermit thrush, spotted sandpiper, white-crowned sparrow, lincoln sparrow, blue grouse, western flycatcher, Williamson's sapsucker, sharp-skinned hawk, hairy woodpecker, and Clark's nutcracker.

Mammals: Marten, mink, perhaps a few black bear, long-tailed weasel, marmot, mule deer, and snowshoe rabbit.

CANADIAN (MONTANE) ZONE. 8,000 feet to 10,000 feet altitude. Corresponds to 50° to 60° N. Lat.

Trees: Great forests of Englemann spruce, Douglas fir and lodgepole pine. The Colorado blue spruce grows well in this zone as do aspens and some juniper and ponderosa pines. Along the streams are willows, water birches, narrow-leafed cottonwood and thinleaf alder.

Flowers: Most varieties grow best in the aspen groves, near streams, in the open conifer forests, or the open mountain parks. Spring brings the fairy slipper, monkshood, marsh marigold, dandelion, and white phlox. The warmer summer months find a great variety of wild flowers in bloom, including mariposa lily, glacier lily, nodding onion, Rocky Mountain iris, anemone, showy loco, strawberry blight, goldenrod, woolly mullein, columbine, globeflower, Oregon grape, wallflower, rosecrown, strawberries, raspberries, shrub cinquefoil, lodgepole lupine, cranesbill, fireweed, kinnikinnick, wood beauty, shooting star, Parry's primrose, green gentian, fringed gentian, scarlet gilia, purple fringe, tall chiming bell, Indian paintbrushes, little red elephant, cutleaf daisy and cow parsley. Before frost, the bistort, larkspur, stonecrop, yarrow, asters, daisies and gentians will be found.

Birds: Blue grouse, olive-sided flycatcher, mountain chickadee, red-breasted nuthatch, Townsend's solitaire, red-naped sapsucker, downy woodpecker, house wren, tree swallow, warbling vireo, ruby-crowned kinglet, white-crowned sparrow, Western tanager, pine siskin, water ouzel (dipper), mountain bluebird, Cooper's hawk, raven and Stellar's jay.

Mammals: Mule deer, elk, yellow-bellied marmot, porcupine, beaver, otter, bobcat, red fox, mountain lion, Richardson's ground squirrel, chipmunk, (golden mantled ground squirrel), pack rat, pine squirrel, Fremont's squirrel, long-tailed weasel, coyote, and the deer mouse.

TRANSITION (FOOTHILLS) ZONE. 6,000 feet to 8,000 feet altitude. Corresponds to 40° to 50° N. Lat.

Trees: Ponderosa (Western yellow pine) is the most common conifer in the lower one-half of the Canadian Zone and extending into the Transition Zone. The narrow-leafed cottonwood and balsam poplar are common along streams. Gambel oak (scrub oak) and mountain mahogany often cover hillsides, sometimes in very dense thickets. Rocky Mountain juniper and pinon pine are common in this zone, and aspens sometimes reach down from the higher elevations. Gooseberry, dogwood, hawthorn, chokecherry, thimbleberry, squawbush, and buffalo berry are prominent shrubs.

Flowers: Spring flowers that are common in this zone include the Rocky Mountain iris, Oregon grape, bleeding heart, serviceberry, strawberry, chokecherry, kinnikinnick, shooting star, dandelion, sand lily, cut-leafed daisy, white phlox, paintbrush, candytuft, Lambert's loco, pasque flower and penstemons. Summer blossoms include cattails, mariposa lily, wild lily-of-the-valley, bistort, columbine, yucca, larkspur, globeflower, wallflower, stonecrop, shrub cinquefoil, wild rose, locoweed, lodgepole lupine, cranesbill, fireweed, evening primrose, yellow evening primrose, green gentian, scarlet gilia, purple fringe, Wyoming paintbrush, little red elephant, penstemons woolly mullein, harebell, yarrow, showy aster, thistles, cutleaf daisy, showy daisy, brown-eyed susan, sunflowers, stickweed, Easter daisy, miner's candle, raspberry, twinflower, buttercup and wood beauty. Fall flowers are mainly mountain sorrel, clematis, Rocky Mountain beeplant, sagebrush, asters, sunflowers, rabbitbrush and goldenrod.

Birds: Steller's jay, mountain bluebird, pygmy nuthatch, chickadee, Western tanager, belted kingfisher, magpie, pine siskin, water ouzel (dipper), canon wren, rock wren, Brewer's blackbird, red-winged blackbird, grackle, Western meadowlark, marsh hawk, Western red-tailed hawk, and raven.

Mammals: Pine squirrel, mule deer, striped skunk, thirteen-lined ground squirrel, porcupine, badger, tuft-eared squirrel, muskrat, prairie dog, least chipmunk, coyote and cotton-tail rabbit.

UPPER SONORAN (PLAINS) ZONE. 4,500 to 6,000 feet altitude. Corresponds to 30° to 40° N. Lat.

Trees: Cottonwoods, willows, box elders are common. Some ponderosa pine and scrub oak are found on the north-facing slopes.

Flowers: Most common springtime flowers are cattail, mariposa lily, wild lily-of-the-valley, Rocky Mountain iris, pasque flower, sand lily, yucca, larkspur, globeflower, bleeding heart, wallflower, serviceberry, wild rose, locoweed, cranesbill, fireweed, evening primrose, shooting star, scarlet gilia, yarrow, Indian paintbrush, Easter daisy and buttercup. Summer flowers that are usually in abundance include mountain sorrel, bistort, cactus, Rocky Mountain beeplant, stonecrop, shrub cinquefoil, bluebonnet, locoweed, golden banner, yellow evening primrose, milkweed, morning glory, woolly mullein, harebell, sagebrush, showy aster, thistle, brown-eyed susan, sunflowers and stickweed. Fall colors on the plains are principally rabbitbrush, clematis gone to seed, sunflowers, asters, wild gourds, goldenrod and sagebrush.

Birds: Rock wren, Western red-tailed hawk, Western meadowlark, magpie, and sparrow hawk.

Mammals: Jack rabbit, thirteen-lined ground squirrel, prairie dog and coyote.

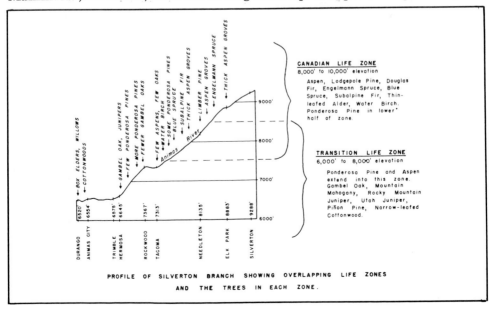

PROFILE OF SILVERTON BRANCH SHOWING OVERLAPPING LIFE ZONES AND THE TREES IN EACH ZONE.

Engine 497 in the Durango yards in May 1983. All that remained to be done is to install new flues and to pass an ICC boiler inspection before the engine can be put back together and to "hang the jewelry in place" (install the air pump, headlight, bell, whistle, and piping). When this photo was taken, the cab, frame and running gear had a new coat of red-oxide primer; the boiler, domes and tanks were newly coated with aluminum paint. (F. W. Osterwald)

Engine 497 went into regular service on the D&SNG during the summer of 1984. All of the flues were inspected and 95 were replaced. The boiler jacket and lagging were also replaced. The running gear was in good shape and required little work. On June 6, 1984, an historic and noteworthy event took place when K-37 engine 497 made its first trip to Silverton. This was the first time any K-37 had run on the Silverton Branch. The extra, non-revenue, mixed train included two boxcars, two coaches, a concession car and a caboose. On June 15, 1984 engine 497 went into regular service.

Engine 497 standing in Silverton June 6, 1984.   (Photo courtesy Robert E. Emmett)

The D&SNG acquired ex-Rio Grande Southern engine 42 in 1983, and it finally returned to Durango after an absence of 31 years. This Baldwin was one of six 2-8-0 engines built in 1887 for the D&RG (class C-17) and was originally numbered 420. In November 1916, the engine was sold to the RGS and used until the railroad was dismantled in 1952. The last train movement on the RGS consisted of engine 42 with a caboose running from Grady, which is east of Mancos, to Durango. In 1953, the engine was sold to the Narrow Gauge Motel in Alamosa. During 1958, the 42 was sold to Magic Mountain Amusement Park at Golden, Colo., where it was converted to burn fuel oil and was operated briefly. In 1969, it was sold to the Woodmoor Corp. at Monument, Colo. It came back to Golden in 1971 as part of a restaurant display at Heritage Square until it was rescued by the D&SNG. The engine weighed 35¼ tons and pulled with 17,100 pounds of effort when new.

Ex-Rio Grande Southern engine 42 outside the Durango roundhouse in May, 1983, soon after its arrival. *(F. W. Osterwald)*

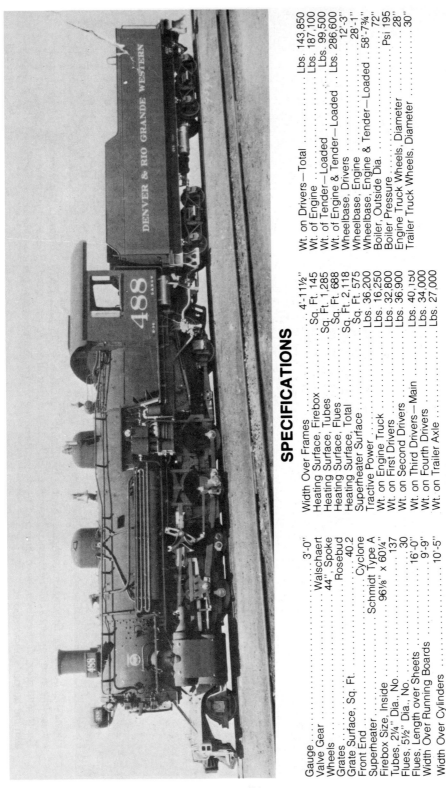

SPECIFICATIONS

Gauge	3'-0"
Valve Gear	Walschaert
Wheels	44", Spoke
Grates	Rosebud
Grate Surface, Sq. Ft.	40.2
Front End	Cyclone
Superheater	Schmidt Type A
Firebox Size, Inside	96⅛" x 60¼"
Tubes, 2¼" Dia., No.	137
Flues, 5½" Dia., No.	30
Flues, Length over Sheets	16'-0"
Width Over Running Boards	9'-9"
Width Over Cylinders	10'-5"
Width Over Frames	4'-11½"
Heating Surface, Firebox	Sq. Ft. 145
Heating Surface, Tubes	Sq. Ft. 1,285
Heating Surface, Flues	Sq. Ft. 688
Heating Surface, Total	Sq. Ft. 2,118
Superheater Surface	Sq. Ft. 575
Tractive Power	Lbs. 36,200
Wt. on Engine Truck	Lbs. 16,250
Wt. on First Drivers	Lbs. 32,800
Wt. on Second Drivers	Lbs. 36,900
Wt. on Third Drivers—Main	Lbs. 40,150
Wt. on Fourth Drivers	Lbs. 34,000
Wt. on Trailer Axle	Lbs. 27,000
Wt. on Drivers—Total	Lbs. 143,850
Wt. of Engine	Lbs. 187,100
Wt. of Tender—Loaded	Lbs. 99,500
Wt. of Engine & Tender—Loaded	Lbs. 286,600
Wheelbase, Drivers	12'-3"
Wheelbase, Engine	28'-1"
Wheelbase, Engine & Tender—Loaded	58'-7¾"
Boiler, Outside Dia.	72"
Boiler Pressure	Psi 195
Engine Truck Wheels, Diameter	28"
Trailer Truck Wheels, Diameter	30"

Photo and specifications for K-36 engine 488, built in 1925 for the D&RGW. (Colorado Historical Society)

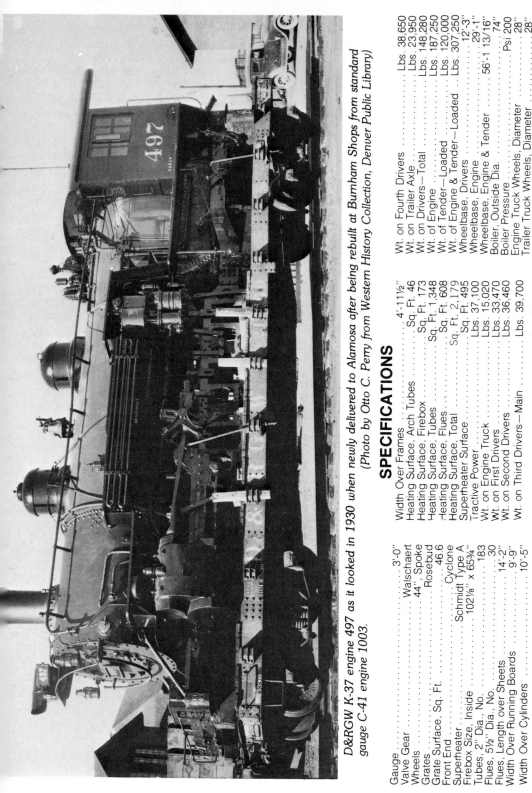

D&RGW K-37 engine 497 as it looked in 1930 when newly delivered to Alamosa after being rebuilt at Burnham Shops from standard gauge C-41 engine 1003.
(Photo by Otto C. Perry from Western History Collection, Denver Public Library)

SPECIFICATIONS

Gauge	3'-0"
Valve Gear	Walschaert
Wheels	44" Spoke
Grates	Rosebud
Grate Surface, Sq. Ft.	46.6
Front End	Cyclone
Superheater	Schmidt Type A
Firebox Size, Inside	102⅛" x 65¾"
Tubes, 2" Dia., No.	183
Flues, 5½" Dia., No.	30
Flues, Length over Sheets	14'-2"
Width Over Running Boards	9'-9"
Width Over Cylinders	10'-5"
Width Over Frames	4'-11½"
Heating Surface, Arch Tubes	Sq. Ft. 46
Heating Surface, Firebox	Sq. Ft. 173
Heating Surface, Tubes	Sq. Ft. 1,348
Heating Surface, Flues	Sq. Ft. 608
Heating Surface, Total	Sq. Ft. 2,179
Superheater Surface	Sq. Ft. 495
Tractive Power	Lbs. 37,100
Wt. on Engine Truck	Lbs. 15,020
Wt. on First Drivers	Lbs. 33,470
Wt. on Second Drivers	Lbs. 36,460
Wt. on Third Drivers—Main	Lbs. 39,700
Wt. on Fourth Drivers	Lbs. 38,650
Wt. on Trailer Axle	Lbs. 23,950
Wt. on Drivers—Total	Lbs. 148,280
Wt. of Engine	Lbs. 187,250
Wt. of Tender—Loaded	Lbs. 120,000
Wt. of Engine & Tender—Loaded	Lbs. 307,250
Wheelbase, Drivers	12'-3"
Wheelbase, Engine	29'-1"
Wheelbase, Engine & Tender	56'-1 13/16"
Boiler, Outside Dia.	74"
Boiler Pressure	Psi 200
Engine Truck Wheels, Diameter	28"
Trailer Truck Wheels, Diameter	28"

CARS

The cars used on the Silverton trains, although they all appear to be similar in external appearance, had long and varied careers in service on the Rio Grande. They were built at many different times by different builders and have undergone numerous and extensive rebuildings and renumberings. Some have survived train wrecks and fires in the past, and others were once converted to outfit (work) cars and then have been revived for passenger service. A few were idle for many years until rescued by the D&SNG, extensively rebuilt in the new Durango carshop, and returned to service. The origins of some cars are obscure and difficult to determine. Histories of the various cars given below were assembled from many sources, but much of the information was compiled by Jackson C. Thode from data in the D&RGW files.

The oldest car used regularly on **The Silverton** trains (and as far as is known, the second oldest railroad car in Colorado) is D&SNG car 212. This car was built by Billmeyer and Small in 1879 as a coach named the "Caliente" and its original number was 20. At that time it had a seating capacity of 45. It was rebuilt in 1887 into a combination coach-baggage car and was renumbered 215. At that time it had a clerestory roof with bullnose ends and a seating capacity of 23. The interior of the passenger compartment was finished in ash and the baggage compartment was painted a light green. It underwent some later changes, however, because by 1904 the clerestory roof had duckbill ends and there were seats for 28 passengers. In 1923 the car, together with most other D&RGW narrow gauge passenger equipment, was rebuilt and the original 28-inch wheels were replaced with 26-inch wheels.

The car served the Pagosa Springs Branch of the D&RGW for many years and during that service a caboose cupola, end ladders and roof walks were added for mixed train use, as well as high handrails along the roof walks. When the Pagosa Springs Branch was abandoned, the cupola was removed and the handrails and roof walk extended for the full length of the car. The car was then assigned to the Silverton Branch. In an interesting turn of events, D&RGW car 215 became 212. Combination car 215 had been sold by the Rio Grande to a Mexican railroad in 1942, but when the D&RGW discovered that 215 was larger than the other narrow gauge combine, 212, the numbers of the two cars were switched and the smaller car was sent to Mexico.

In 1950 the 212 and coaches 306, 320 and 280 were painted yellow-orange (now known as "Rio Grande Gold") for the movie, "Ticket to Tomahawk," which was filmed mostly on the Silverton Branch. At that time the high handrail on the roof was removed. Shortly thereafter 212 became the entire consist of a stub train that ran between Chama and Dulce, New Mexico. This train was operated for a few months after passenger service between Alamosa and Durango was discontinued because the New Mexico Public Utilities Commission refused permission to abandon in that state. After abandonment of the stub train, 212 returned to **The Silverton.** In 1964 the car was converted at the Burnham Shops to a snack-bar car. The old interior was stripped and a lunch counter, four-burner hot-plate, LP gas system, soft drink ice-cooling tank, overhead water tank, floor racks and drain system were installed. The underframe was rebuilt and the running gear overhauled at the same time. Number 212 was converted to a coach and given new steel siding at Burnham in 1979. The coach seats were removed to provide more space for the snack-bar by the D&SNG.

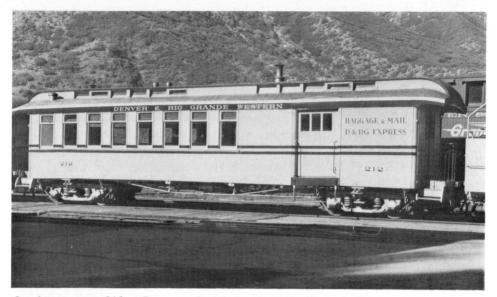

Combination car 212 at Durango, September 4, 1951. The new "Rio Grande Gold" paint job was done for the movie, "Ticket to Tomahawk." Coupled to the baggage end of 212 is the glass-topped observation car, "Silver Vista." (F. W. Osterwald)

Coach 312 was built by the D&RG in 1887. It replaced another coach, also numbered 312, which had originally been number 88. The car had a clerestory roof with bullnose ends, as it does today. The interior was finished in ash and the car seated 46 passengers. The carbody was lowered, the underframe reinforced, extension side bearings applied and 26-inch wheels substituted for the original 30-inch wheels in 1923. The car was rebuilt at Alamosa in 1937 with closed vestibule ends, train-line steam heat instead of a coal stove, electric lights and deluxe Heywood-Wakefield reclining coach seats for 24 passengers. In this configuration the car was used on the deluxe **San Juan** and **Shavano** trains (the **Shavano** was operated between Salida and Gunnison). Storm sashes were applied to the windows in 1940. Further remodeling in 1957 for service on **The Silverton** resulted in floors that were covered by ¼ inch rubber and pneumatic tile and tramway (bus) seats for 46 passengers. A new "Rio Grande Gold" paint job replaced the coach green. New windows and scribed steel sides were added at the D&RGW Burnham shops in 1979.

Coach 319 was built in 1882 by Jackson and Sharp. Its original number was 95 and it had a clerestory roof and bullnose ends. The car had 30-inch paper-core wheels and seated 45 passengers. It became number 319 in 1886. The interior was finished in ash and mahogany. One additional seat apparently was added before 1904. The car was "lowered" (see data on Coach 312) in 1922. It was rebuilt at Alamosa in 1937 with vestibuled ends, steam heat, electric lights and 24 deluxe Heywood-Wakefield reclining coach seats for service on the **San Juan** and **Shavano** deluxe trains. Storm sash was added to the windows in 1940. In 1957 the car was remodeled with rubber and pneumatic tile floor, and bus seats for 46 passengers were added for use on **The Silverton**. The car was repainted with "Rio Grande Gold" at this time. In 1978 the Burnham Shop in Denver installed new windows and scribed steel sides in place of the original wood sides.

97

Car 323 bears the same number it did when built by the D&RG in 1887, and has the same type clerestory roof with bullnose ends as it did then. The interior is finished in ash; the original seating capacity was 46. The car was "lowered" in 1923. It was rebuilt in 1937 at Alamosa with vestibuled ends, train-line steam heat, electric lights, and deluxe reclining seats for 24 persons, for use on the **San Juan** and **Shavano**. Storm sash was applied to the windows in 1940. It was remodeled in 1957 with new flooring, bus seats and a "Rio Grande Gold" paint job for use on **The Silverton.**

Coach 327 was also built in 1887 by the D&RG with configuration very similar to that of coach 312. Its history of various rebuildings is identical to coaches 312, 319 and 323. It was rebuilt with new windows and scribed steel siding instead of wood at Burnham Shops in 1978.

Car 350 had an extremely varied career. The car was built in 1880 by Jackson and Sharp as Horton chair car number 25, carrying the name "Hidalgo," which reflected the original Rio Grande management's interest in a rail connection with Mexico. At that time the car seated 25 people. It was changed to chair car 403 in 1885. In 1919 it was rebuilt into an office and living car for members of the Valuation Survey who were inventorying the entire railroad property after it was returned to private ownership following World War I. The car was lowered and the wheels changed to 26-inch in 1924 when it was converted into a parlor-smoker car. After another rebuilding in 1937 it emerged as a parlor-buffet car named "Alamosa" (with no number) to replace the original "Alamosa" which was destroyed by fire in a derailment on the Rio Grande Southern in 1912. When rebuilt, the car had a closed front vestibule, ash interior, steam heat, electric lights, kitchen and buffet and swivelled, overstuffed seats for 14 passengers for service on the **San Juan.** In 1957 the kitchen and buffet were removed and the car converted to a coach for service on **The Silverton.** It was renumbered 350 in 1959, and was rebuilt with steel siding at Burnham in 1978. The name "Alamosa" was restored soon after the railroad was acquired by the D&SNG, and during the fall of 1981 the car was re-converted to a parlor car with a bar and small oak tables and chairs for 28 passengers (page 131). It is carpeted and equipped with electric lights. As an extra fare car, it is a regular part of trains 261 and 262 (**Cascade Canyon Mixed**) which operate from Durango to Cascade Canyon wye, as well as trains 115 and 116, the revived **San Juan Express** to Silverton.

Coaches 330, 331, 332, 333, 334, 335, 336 and 337 are slightly different than the others, being constructed of steel with sides scribed to represent wood. They were built by the D&RGW at the Burnham Shops in Denver. Numbers 330 and 331 were built in 1963, being the first new narrow gauge cars to be built in the U.S. since the early 1900's. The remainder of the cars were built in 1964. Except for the steel sides and aluminum window frames, they follow the specifications of the older cars very closely. The end platforms are fitted with end posts and ornate guard railings, which, as shown in the photos on page 99, are slightly different from those on older coaches. The cars are heated by coal stoves. The trucks on 330 and 331 are old-timers taken from former Railway Post Office cars X66 and X122. The floors are rubber and pneumatic tile and the seats are the ubiquitous tramway variety. In 1982 the masonite paneling below the windows was removed by the D&SNG, insulation was installed and oak paneling substituted. The cars are all electrically lighted.

The end platform of coach 350 in June, 1965, showing the simple railings and marker lights. This coach, now parlor car "Alamosa", was built in 1880. (F. W. Osterwald)

End platform of coach 331, built in 1963 by the D&RGW Burnham Shops in Denver, showing the ornate railings and bullnose end of the roof. Compare with the photo above of coach 350. (F. W. Osterwala)

Car 257 was built in 1880 by Jackson and Sharp as coach 43 for the D&RG. When delivered it had duckbill roof ends, but these were covered to resemble bullnose ends when the car was rebuilt in 1886 and renumbered 267. In May 1891, it was sold to the Rio Grande Southern Railroad. The RGS again rebuilt the car and renumbered it 257. It was used as a coach until some time in the 1920's, at which time it was converted into a passenger-baggage combination car with two narrow side doors, leaving only about ⅓ of it for people; the windows in the baggage portion were covered. At the same time the underframe and truss-rods were strengthened to carry heavier loads. No. 257 was retired when the RGS began to operate its famous "Galloping Geese" (gasoline-powered railcars) in 1931. For many years it sat beside the roundhouse in Ridgway, Colo., in use only for parts storage, until the RGS was abandoned in 1951. The car sat on a farm near Montrose, Colo. until 1977, when William Jones bought it and moved it to Silverton. The D&SNG bought the car from Mr. Jones in August 1983, and following a complete re-building, it was returned to service in 1986 as coach 257, named "Bell."

Car 270 was built in 1880 at the Delaware Car Works of Jackson and Sharp, Wilmington, Delaware and named "Galesteo." It originally cost $3,198.42. The car's original number was 46 but it was renumbered 270 in 1886 and was transferred from revenue to non-revenue work service in 1924. It became a kitchen-diner outfit car, with extension side-bearings applied to the trucks, and was renumbered 0270 also in 1924. At the time of the Valuation Survey in 1920 the interior was described as painted wood, ash and walnut, with crimson plush seats. It had two coal stoves for heat. The car was rebuilt at Durango by the D&SNG in 1983, at which time the interior was restored to its original condition except for the floor and seats. As with all cars rebuilt by the D&SNG it is fully insulated for winter use. The interior has birds-eye maple panels between the windows. Portions of the original oak and mahogany moldings were preserved and other new ones were milled to match. All were very carefully reinstalled above the windows. Buntin-type reversible seats were redesigned and fabricated by the D&SNG for this coach, using an original Buntin seat in an old work car as a model. The car is named "Pinkerton."

D&RGW outfit car 0270, now D&SNG coach 270, as it looked in February, 1969 in the Durango yards when used as a kitchen-diner outfit car. (R. W. Osterwald)

Interior of coach 270 in Feb. 1982, soon after D&SNG crews started to remove old wood in preparation for insulating and repaneling.   (All carshop photos, F. W. Osterwald)

End view of coach 270 in the Durango car shop. The underframe and sagging end platform were completely rebuilt and the trucks, in the foreground, overhauled.   (F. W. Osterwald)

101

In May 1983, the D&SNG purchased two cars from the Black Hills Central Railroad in South Dakota. Car 64 is a combination mail-baggage built by the D&RG in March, 1889, and coach 460 is the only narrow gauge tourist-sleeper remaining from a group built in 1886. This coach, assigned to work service in the early 1900's, was used on a D&RGW wrecking train as late as 1957 before it was sold to the BHC Railroad.

Concession car 566, according to Jackson C. Thode, "is a story all by itself, which has to be put together piecemeal." The early D&RG records are difficult to interpret, because in 1883 cars were designated as express, baggage and mail, with each category starting with the number one. In 1886 these designations were changed to express, baggage, postal, and combined mail-baggage-express, in which not all the early designations of individual cars carried through to the later designations because of rebuildings, renumberings, scrappings and destruction by accidents. When former D&RGW outfit car 0566 was being rebuilt by the D&SNG in 1982, the number 14 was discovered on the underframe beams above the trucks. The original configuration was found to be that of a four-door postal car when the old siding was removed. According to D&RGW records the original mail cars number 14 to 21 were changed to postal cars and renumbered by 1886. During this renumbering, mail car 14 became postal car number 1 — but this didn't last long as it was rebuilt to excursion car 566, probably about 1888, at which time the four side-doors were removed and seats and windows added. As an excursion car it was divided into two compartments with a table, desk and two bunks. It was renumbered 0566 in July 1904, and changed from passenger to work service in 1914. When inventoried by the Valuation Survey in 1920, it was listed as a Bridge and Building Dept. Foreman coach outfit car. Car 566 probably was originally mail car 14, built in 1882 by the D&RG, using iron work from Billmeyer and Small of York, Pa. for a total cost of $3,128.41.

Badly weathered D&RGW outfit car 0566, now D&SNG concession car 566 at Durango in February, 1969.   *(R. W. Osterwald)*

Although the interior of the new Durango car shop was not completed in Feb. 1982, carmen were busy reconditioning, insulating and refinishing D&SNG concession car 566. To insulate the car, all the siding had to be removed and replaced. The original oak center-sill was replaced with steel and the car was completely reinforced. *(F. W. Osterwald)*

Postmark, probably from the wrapper of a bundle of mail, found in 1982 behind the interior paneling of car 566 when it was being rebuilt by the D&SNG.

Interior of car 566, which was given new plywood flooring and paneling. The original four-door postal car configuration is apparent. *(F. W. Osterwald)*

Car 126 was built by the D&RG in 1883 as baggage car 27. It was re-numbered 126 in 1886; at that time it had a clerestory roof with one baggage door per side and no end doors. It was lowered, the underframe reinforced and extension side bearings installed in 1923. Train-line steam heat, air and signal lines were added in 1939 so the car could be used on the **San Juan** and **Shavano.** The Burnham Shops converted it into a snack-bar car in 1963, at which time the underframe was rebuilt and the running gear overhauled. The D&RGW considered converting it into a coach in 1963, and finally did so in 1979 when steel siding, seats and windows were added. The D&SNG has reconverted the coach to a permanent concession car.

D&RGW baggage car 126 at Durango, September 4, 1951. The "Rio Grande Gold" paint was applied for the movie, "Ticket to Tomahawk," but the letterboard at the top had not yet been lettered "Denver & Rio Grande Western." Compare with photo of car 212 on page 97.
(F. W. Osterwald)

Coach 291 was built by Jackson and Sharp in 1881, as D&RG Railway coach 67 without a name. It was renumbered 291 in 1886 and to 0291 in 1924 when it was transferred to non-revenue work service. The original cost was $3,396.64. When inventoried by the Valuation Survey in 1920 the interior was finished in oak and it contained 22 Buntin seats upholstered in crimson plush. There were two coal stoves for heating. The car was completely rebuilt in 1984. Named the "King Mine," it has seats that duplicate the old fashioned reversible ("walk-over") seats used in coaches a hundred years ago.

Car 311 was built in 1881 by Jackson and Sharp as D&RG coach 87 with a seating capacity of 44 passengers. It too was subjected to renumbering in 1887. The interior was finished in oak, and contained 22 Buntin reversible seats, continuous hat racks, oil lamps and "one large cooler." The car had Pullman steel-plated wooden trucks with 26-inch wheels. The carbody and platforms were lowered, the underframes reinforced and extension side bearings applied at Alamosa in 1922. Although the original cost was $3,575.35, it was sold in 1944 to the Montezuma Lumber Co. at McPhee, Colorado (near Dolores) for $671.00, which was 10 cents less than the appraised value at that time. The car later was sold again and used as a residence. Then it was purchased by Bob Shank of Hermosa, Colorado who in turn sold the coach to the D&SNG in 1982.

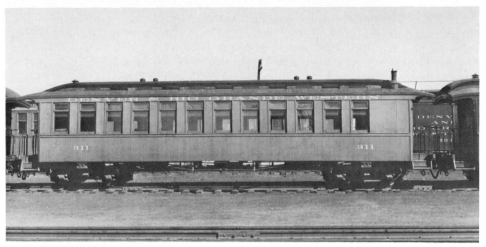

D&RGW coach 311 at Alamosa in 1939, when it was painted coach green. Compare the clerestory roof with duckbill ends to the coach coupled to the right; it has a roof with bullnose ends. (Turner Van Nort)

Coaches 284 and 327 in the Durango yards, September 4, 1951, still wore their Pullman green paint for service on the recently abandoned "San Juan Express". Coach 284 is now preserved at the Colorado Railroad Museum in Golden; coach 327 is now in service on the D&SNG, named the "Durango". (F. W. Osterwald)

Three new "scratch-built" coaches, numbers 630, the "Hunt," 631, the "North Star" and 632, the "Tefft," were added to the roster in 1984 and 1986. The steel underframes, sides and superstructures were built by the Telluride Iron Works in Durango; all other work was done by the D&SNG carmen. These cars have steel sides that are scribed to resemble wood.

Open observation cars 400, 401 and 402 were originally standard gauge D&RGW boxcars 67191, 66665 and 66271. In 1953 these boxcars were converted into pipe cars Nos. 9609, 9611 and 9605 respectively, by cutting down and bracing the sides, removing the ends and adding narrow gauge trucks. As pipe cars they were used between Alamosa and Farmington, N.M. during the oil and gas boom of the 1950's in the San Juan Basin. The cars were converted into observation cars by equipping them with passenger car trucks, steel roofs, tile floors and tramway seats in 1963. Three additional open observation cars, 403, 404 and 405 were built in the Burnham Shops for the 1967 season of **The Silverton.** These were converted from pipe cars 9606, 9600 and 9601, respectively, which were also originally D&RGW standard gauge boxcars in the 66000-66999 series. The trucks for these three cars came from coaches 284, 306 and 320 which were sold to the Colorado Railroad Museum in Golden, Colorado. Open observation cars 411 and 412 were built between 1982 and 1985 by the Durango carshop of the D&SNG from pipe cars 9603 and 9608.

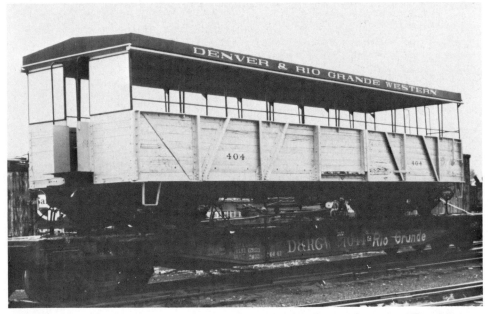

Car 404, one of three new open observation cars built in Denver for use on The Silverton. *This photo was taken May 29, 1967 in Alamosa, shortly after the car was delivered on a standard gauge flatcar. It went to Durango June 12, 1967 with the first westbound narrow gauge freight of that season.* (D. B. Osterwald)

Between 1982 and 1986, eleven new open observation cars were built by the D&SNG (see Roster, page 150). Fourteen pairs of passenger trucks were built in 1983 for the new cars and also to replace worn sets on some of the older equipment. Look for the new D&SNG stamp on the sides.

Combination car 213, named the "Home Ranch," was entirely "scratch built" in 1983. It was especially designed so that passengers in wheelchairs can ride **The Silverton.** Telluride Iron Works in Durango fabricated the steel frame and sides, using D&RGW plans for the cars built during the 1960's. D&SNG car shop personnel completed the car with wooden paneling inside and wood siding outside. The car is insulated for winter use, has a kitchen-concession **area** and a large restroom at one end, and 26 removable seats in the passenger section. Sliding doors on each side, equivalent to baggage doors on conventional coach-baggage combines, have hydraulic lifts to handle wheelchairs. Extra-wide aisles and hand rails make this car ideal for handicapped **patrons.**

D&SNG combination passenger-baggage car 213, the "Home Ranch", gets lots of enthusiastic use by passengers in wheel chairs. Here, Mr. Ray Vidrine of Poway, California is aided by Conductor John Garrefa (left), and brakemen Dan Bartch (behind) and David Martinez (right).   *(D. B. Osterwald)*

The rolling stock of the D&SNG also includes RailCamp Car, 3681, an ex-D&RGW boxcar that was rebuilt to D&SNG standards in 1984. The interior was refurbished to accommodate six people and is equipped with a kitchen, a bathroom and beds for four people. This car can be rented for up to five days and is pulled to a siding in the upper Animas Canyon by an extra train. It's a great way for a quiet vacation, fishing and watching trains!

PRIVATE CARS

General William Jackson Palmer

Business Car B-7 was built in 1880 by the Burnham Shops of the D&RG as a flat-roofed baggage car, using ironwork from Billmeyer and Small at York, Pennsylvania. The total cost of the car was $1,769.43. In 1885 it was numbered 116, but the following year it was rebuilt for use as a paycar and given the number "R". It is believed that the clerestory roof was added in 1886. The car was lowered in 1930. In 1946 the B-7 and B-2 (now the "Cinco Animas") made a last official trip over the entire Rio Grande Southern Railroad with noted authors Lucius Beebe and Charles Clegg as guests. During still another rebuilding at the Burnham Shops in 1963, the underframe and trucks were modernized and strengthened, the kitchen was remodelled, a "Rio Grande Gold" paint job was added and the car renamed the "General William Jackson Palmer" in honor of the founder of the Denver and Rio Grande Railway. The car is now owned by the D&SNG and will be used as a business car when repaired. It also has the distinction of being the oldest business car owned and operated by any U.S. railroad.

Nomad

The "Nomad" (car B-3) was built in 1878 by Billmeyer and Small at York, Pennsylvania, as a Horton Chair Car. It was numbered 16 and named "Fairplay" until 1886 when it was rebuilt by the D&RG and designated business car "N". The car was then part of an Executive Office Train consisting of a kitchen-provision car, and two dining, sleeping and observation cars. This Executive Train carried President Taft to the dedication of the Gunnison Diversion Tunnel west of Montrose, Colorado in 1909. In 1912 the car was renumbered B-2, a designation that did not last very long. In January, 1917 the B-2, together with B-1 and B-3, were part of a special train of important financiers en route to Durango after inspecting various mining properties near Silverton. At Bell's Spur the entire train, known as the "Million Dollar Special," turned over. Car B-2 was at the rear of the train and is reported to have slid 50 feet down the mountain. The other two cars were completely burned, but no one was hurt. The interior of the B-2 was remodelled as an officer's sleeping car at the Burnham Shops and the car renumbered B-3 in 1917, the number B-2 being assigned at that time to the present "Cinco Animas." Twenty-six inch wheels were installed in 1930. The car was exhibited at the 1949 Chicago Railroad Fair and renamed "General Wm. J. Palmer" for the occasion. The car was part of an entire narrow gauge train from the D&RGW, which was lettered for an imaginary Cripple Creek and Tincup Railroad. The B-3 was sold by the D&RGW to a private individual in 1951 and after being sold several more times and extensive remodelling in 1957, it was repainted a deep Pullman green and renamed the "Nomad" sometime between 1958 and 1962. It is the oldest private car now in service in the U.S. This car was also owned by the Cinco Animas Corporation until 1982 when it was sold to the D&SNG Railroad.

Cinco Animas

The "Cinco Animas" was built in 1883 by D&RG carmen in Denver at the Burnham Shop as an emigrant sleeper, numbered 103. Emigrant sleepers on the narrow gauge had odd configurations internally, with 30 seats below and berths above. Sometime later it was renumbered 452, still as an emigrant sleeper. By 1904, 452 (ex-103) was redesignated as a tourist car, possibly with the same internal configuration. Later it was renumbered 0452 for use as an outfit car. In 1909 outfit car 0452 was damaged in a wreck on the Rio Grande Southern Railroad. About the same time, a paycar, numbered "F", was also badly damaged in a wreck. Because the railroad employees needed to be paid as soon as possible, the 0452 carbody was refitted internally as a paycar and was placed on the running gear and other parts from ex-paycar "F". When all the repairs were finished and the cars returned to service, the original 0452 had been numbered "F" and "F", which was outfitted with running gear from 0452, then became 0452. The original "F" carbody, now outfit car 0452, is on the Cumbres & Toltec Scenic Railroad at Chama, N.M.

In 1913 car "F" (ex-0452) became B-5 and was used extensively on both the standard and narrow gauge lines of the D&RG by changing the trucks at Montrose, Colorado. The car was rebuilt again at the Burnham Shops in 1917 and renumbered B-2 to replace a car destroyed by fire during a derailment at Bell's Spur near Rockwood. It was then assigned to an official train. Vestibules were added to both ends about 1924 and 26-inch wheels replaced the 28-inch wheels in 1930. The car was sold by the D&RGW in 1954 and moved to Oklahoma. In 1963 the car was purchased by the Cinco Animas Corporation and returned to Colorado. At that time the vestibule was removed from the observation room end, an open platform with railings was added, and new Tuscan red paint was applied at the Burnham Shops. The car then received its present name, "Cinco Animas", for the five individuals who jointly purchased the car, and returned it to Durango. In 1982 the corporation sold the car to the D&SNG; it is available for charter trips on the Silverton trains.

TRACK

Track for the D&RG Silverton Branch was originally laid with light steel rail from the Colorado Coal and Iron Co. at Pueblo, Colorado that weighed 30 pounds to the yard. This was the first steel rail produced at the Pueblo plant of what is now the Colorado Fuel & Iron Co. Ties were untreated native timbers and were rough hewn, not sawed. For the most part, ballast was absent. This trackwork was cheap, but the grade on which it was laid was not. Much of it, particularly in the Animas canyon, was blasted from solid rock. The resulting railroad bed probably was adequate for the light engines and cars that were used at first. It is quite likely that the railroad considered such things as ballast and level track to be luxuries that could be paid for later from operating revenues. No tie plates were used so that rails were spiked directly to the ties (photo page 66).

Most of the original 30-pound rail was replaced by 40- and 52-pound about 1911 to 1917. Shortly thereafter, heavier engines could be used on the line. This rail has now been completely replaced by 85- to 90-pound rail, but much of this rail replacement was very haphazard. Common practice on the Rio Grande narrow gauge, especially in later years, was to replace rails with whatever was handy. Rail replacement by the D&SNG is extensive and systematic. None of the original rail now exists, except possibly in the Durango or Silverton yards, or in the Animas River as a result of flooding!

Maximum horizontal curvature on the line was 30°, which corresponds to a radius of curvature of 190.99 feet. As used by railroad locating engineers, curves are described by the angle at the center of curvature that subtends a chord of 100 feet. Thus radii drawn at the ends of a 100-foot chord drawn to a 30° curve would intersect at an angle of 30°. The sharp curves used by the D&RG in such places as the Animas canyon explain why the railroad was built narrow gauge — it was cheaper to construct. The length of a horizontal curve is also given in degrees, indicating how much of a circular arc is used by the curve.

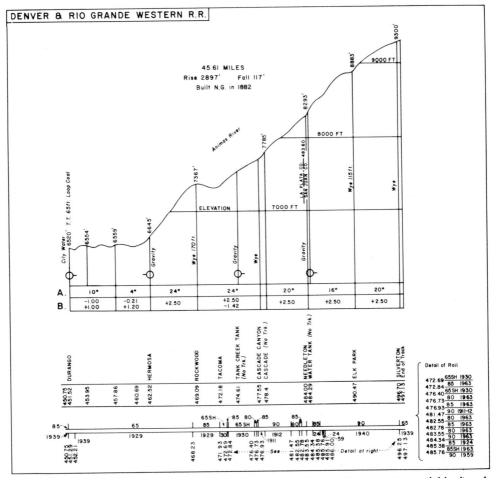

Profile of Silverton Branch. Barred circles indicate where locomotive water is available, line A gives the maximum curvature between the indicated points, and line B gives the maximum grade. Since this profile was drawn, all 65-pound rail has been replaced by 85- and 90-pound rail. (Courtesy Jackson C. Thode)

Maximum grade on the branch is 2.50%, as shown in the above profile. This means that the track rises (or falls) 2.50 feet in elevation for each 100 feet of distance along the rail. Although this is somewhat steep as compared to most mainline railroads, it is gentle compared to the 4% grades on the

110

west side of Cumbres Pass between Antonito, Colo. and Chama, N.M. Four percent grades were common on many of the early narrow gauge lines, but most now have been abandoned.

Track profiles are used by dispatchers and other railroad officials to determine the types of engines and cars that can be used on different parts of the track, where helper engines are required and what kind to use, where passing tracks and sidings are located so that meets and passes can be planned, and where locomotives can get water. It is interesting to note that the D&RGW never had a water tank in Silverton. Maximum curvature indicates what type of cars can be used, and maximum grade lets them know what engines are needed. The weight and type of rail must be taken into account also, so that heavy engines are not allowed to travel on sections with light rail.

A wye was built in 1981 at Cascade Canyon (M.P. 477.5) to turn trains on winter trips and on late afternoon summer excursions. Prefabricated panels of track were assembled in the Durango yards and taken to the site on gondola cars for efficient installation. New passing tracks at Home Ranch Siding (M.P. 457.2) and at Pinkerton Siding (M.P. 465.7), replacing sidings used in the early days of the D&RG, were built to handle the increased 1982 passenger schedules.

In 1986, Pinkerton Siding was lengthened 200 feet to the north, and Tacoma Siding 400 feet to the north. In 1985, the D&SNG purchased the Silverton depot from the San Juan Historical Society, and in 1986 a 1000-foot siding was built where the old scale track was located many years ago.

The original bridges were wooden. Most of the timbers and iron work for these bridges were assembled at Canon City, Colorado, and shipped to Durango. The original bridges have been replaced with more modern ones of either steel or treated wood construction. In addition, most of the larger trestles have been filled in so that less maintenance is required, and greater speeds and loadings are possible. A large curved trestle at M.P. 470.2 burned in 1904 and was replaced by a fill (photo page 33).

Bridge and building yard of the D&RG Railway at Canon City, Colorado in 1882. Bridge timbers were prepared here for use on all parts of the system. The boxcar is on light rail fastened to rough hewn, unballasted ties. *(Colorado Historical Society)*

On May 26, 1981, the first narrow gauge stock extra in many years left Rockwood, hauling horses to Ah! Wilderness Guest Ranch. Several cars of pipes, timbers and other material for the power plant at Tacoma are on a side track waiting to be moved when needed.

(F. W. Osterwald)

Freight business, both large and small, is solicited by the D&SNG. Even before opening day, the line had carried many flat cars of large pipe and other material to the power plant at Tacoma for extensive upgrading undertaken by the Colorado-Ute Electric Association. The D&SNG purchased three stock cars for the express purpose of hauling horses from Rockwood to Ah! Wilderness Guest Ranch. Many years had passed since such extra stock trains were operated on the narrow gauge. During the summer of 1981, equipment was hauled to Exxon Exploration Co. crews along the Animas canyon for their mineral survey work in the Needle Mountains.

Upgrading of the track, roadbed and facilities continues. Much new heavy rail has been installed and thousands of old ties have been replaced. A narrow gauge Pettibone machine (a self-propelled track maintenance unit which can be used as a front-end loader, as a brush-cutter, or as a small crane) was purchased in 1982. Four steel hopper cars were purchased in 1982 from the East Broad Top Railroad in Mount Union, Pa. These cars are used to haul ballast.

A new, modern narrow gauge track-tamping machine was acquired in 1983 and a ballast regulator is now in use. For a few days in May 1985, the line was closed to passenger traffic while major reinforcements were made to stabilize the roadbed along the High Line, (photo page 146).

Three new stalls and a welding shop were added to the Durango roundhouse by December 1984. Four more tracks were laid at the south end of the Durango yards to store work equipment and also cars to be restored and returned to service.

In 1985, another improvement to the rolling stock was the installation of a second separate straight-air brake system, as a back-up for the existing automatic air brake system. According to Dan Nicols, General Car Foreman, this dual braking system not only doubles the safety of the trains, but the cars ride much smoother and the brake shoes last twice as long.

Rocky mountain splendor in the Animas canyon. This lovely view toward the northeast of the Grenadier Range is just south of M.P. 486. The columbines growing beside the rail are Colorado's state flower.

(Richard L. Hunter)

When weary crews had just about finished the back-breaking job of tunneling through the huge slide near the snowshed, the Rio Grande sent George L. Beam, their talented photographer, to record some of the activities in opening the Silverton Branch. This may have been the first engine to start through the tunnel. The white flags on the engine indicate that it is an extra or work train.

This may have been the first scheduled southbound freight train through the snow tunnel. There are no flags on the head engine. The brakemen are standing on the tops of the cars, ready to club down the hand brakes if necessary.

Perhaps this view looking south is of the rear of the freight train shown in the previous photo. Some melting had taken place as the roadbed appears quite dry. One can assume the men were relieved that their labors were over — at least for a few days!
(These three photos by George L. Beam from glass plates in the D&RGW collection.)
(Courtesy of Jackson C. Thode.)

View northward of the interior of the 1906 snow tunnel.   *(Collection of W. D. Joyce)*

Other years when snowslides blocked the Silverton Branch were 1916, 1928 and 1932. In 1932 the job of opening the line seemed almost hopeless, so the work of clearing the track was suspended from February to May. By that time Silverton was not completely dependent upon the railroad for all supplies, food and coal, because Highway 550 was kept open.

The Silverton Branch continued to limp along — its mixed trains carried a few businessmen and some miners and their families to Silverton. Tourists were few; railroad club excursions to the San Juans did not start until the late 1940's and 1950's. Freight trains carried some ore from the Silverton area and limestone from the Rockwood quarry until 1930 when the smelter in Durango closed. During World War II the smelter was reopened by the Vanadium Corp. of America (VCA) to process vanadium and uranium ore. It operated until 1963 when the plant was finally closed and dismantled. The VCA plant did not give any business to the Silverton Branch, however, as most of the ore arrived in Durango either by truck or via the RGS. Only heated protests from local residents kept the line open on a reduced schedule. Mixed trains ran on Sundays, Wednesdays, and Fridays only and in 1949 only 16 trains ran to Silverton. Still, the Silverton Branch survived! Gradually ridership increased. To accommodate the increasing numbers of passengers, in 1947 the Rio Grande built a glass-roofed observation car, the "Silver Vista," but it was burned in a shop fire at Alamosa in 1953.

With the dismantling of the Rio Grande Southern Railroad in 1952, an era of narrow gauge railroading in the San Juans was almost at an end. The D&RGW petitioned the Interstate Commerce Commission (ICC) to abandon the Silverton Branch, but in April, 1962 this request was denied. The railroad then accepted the fact that they were in the business of carrying tourists from Durango to Silverton and return on an unforgettable "Journey to Yesterday." Early in 1963 the Rio Grande purchased a number of old buildings and land surrounding the depot and started a renovation program which resulted in "Rio Grande Land." New stores, gift shops, the General Palmer Hotel and the Grande Palace Restaurant were opened, and a large parking lot was built on the west side of the depot. As ridership continued to increase, new coaches were built in Denver and the second section of **The Silverton** started running in 1963.

On a special occasion in August, 1947, the northbound train stopped after crossing the Animas River below Tacoma, probably to let passengers off for a "photo run-by." All the cars except the "Silver Vista" were painted coach green. Car 126 is behind the engine, followed by combine 212. (*D&RGW collections, Colorado Historical Society*)

120

On Sept. 30, 1947 Otto Perry photographed the Silverton Mixed, train No. 461, near Rockwood. This 13-car train was pulled by K-27 engine 463 with the "Silver Vista" on the rear.
(Denver Public Library, Western History Department)

D&RGW K-27 engine 453 headed north toward Silverton at the south switch of the Hermosa siding, probably in the early 1950's. K-27 engines with these over-size wedge plows were commonly used on the branch before the K-28's became available.
(Collection of Kenneth Logan)

Hidden from passengers riding the Silverton trains is an old locomotive boiler on the hillside northwest of M.P. 477.9. The boiler, once used to power the sawmill at Tefft, is all that is left of engine 32, the "Gold King," of the Silverton, Gladstone and Northerly Railroad (SG&N). Originally, the boiler was part of engine 77, the "Rinconida," purchased new by the D&RG in 1886. The 77 was transferred to the D&RGW Railway in 1886, a line in Utah which later became the Rio Grande Western Railroad. Finally in 1891, 77 was sold to the Rio Grande Southern and renumbered engine 32. Number 32 saw much service on the RGS until 1899 when the engine was sold to the SG&N. The SG&N named the engine "Gold King," but kept the number 32. It was used to haul ore from the Gold King mine at Gladstone, northeast of Silverton, until sometime between 1909 and 1912 when it was dismantled and the boiler shipped to the sawmill. Otto Mears started the sawmill at Tefft after the October, 1911 flood to cut ties and bridge timbers to rebuild the Silverton Branch. Two old coaches, the "Red Mountain" and baggage-coach combine 11, the "Yankee Girl," were moved to Tefft and used as storage buildings at the sawmill. (Richard L. Hunter)

This 1888 combination car, "Red Mountain," had many years service on Mears' Silverton Railroad until it was moved to Tefft. The car was in bad condition when photographed in 1977 and had completely collapsed by 1981. *(Richard L. Hunter)*

Conductor Alva F. Lyons, one of the railroaders who was instrumental in promoting The Silverton as a tourist attraction, never tired of passing out his knowledge of the narrow gauge and of the San Juan country to people on his trains. This view probably was taken in the late 1950's because coach 327 has tramway seats.

(Photo by J. A. Taylor from the Collections in the Museum of N.M.)

In 1949 the movie "Ticket to Tomahawk" was filmed on the Silverton Branch and in Silverton. The depot was renamed "Epitaph" and RGS engine 20 (now at the Colorado Railroad Museum at Golden) became engine 1, The Emma Sweeney).

(Collection of Edna Sanborn)

A head-on collision of D&RGW engines 319 and 345 was staged on the Silverton Branch for the movie, "The Denver & Rio Grande." This scene was filmed July 17, 1951 in the open park at M.P. 475 at what is now Tall Timber Resort. Engine 345, on the right, was renumbered 268 for the collision. Both engines were ruined in this collision and were dismantled in September, 1951.

(Center for Southwest Studies, Ft. Lewis College)

In 1964 the D&RGW constructed a new steel plate girder bridge to replace this old 4-span through truss (3 wooden Howe truss spans, 1 steel truss span) bridge at M.P. 490.0. Details of the original bridge are shown in this photo taken by Richard L. Hunter in 1977.

Details of two spans of the old through truss timber bridge at Elk Park, M.P. 490. Photographed in 1977.   (Richard L. Hunter)

D&RG car foreman and photographer Monte G. Ballough took this view of the Durango yards, looking northwest toward Perin's Peak, about 1910. At this time Durango had both narrow gauge and standard gauge track (3 rails) because the branch to Farmington, N.M., built in 1905, was standard gauge. (Collection of Margaret Ballough Palmer)

View northwest from the hill overlooking the Durango yards. Engine 484 was assembling a work train headed for Flora Vista, N.M. to repair a wash-out on the Farmington Branch, June 28, 1966. (F. W. Osterwald)

Change seems to be a part of railroad history. In May, 1967, the double spout water tank in the Durango yards was torn down and in April, 1968, the coaling tower was demolished to make way for new highway construction. Resulting track realignments gave the Durango yards a new look in 1968, much to the disgust of rail fans. Later, the car shed was torn down so that D&RGW carmen had to work either in the roundhouse or out in the open.

View south showing the double-spout water tank and coaling tower in June, 1966.
(F. W. Osterwald)

To illustrate the many changes in the Durango yards during the past years, compare this photo with the two at the left. By May, 1968, the newly-built loop to turn the Silverton trains cuts across the yard tracks, putting a sharp reverse curve in the roundhouse lead that made access to the house very difficult for engines.
(F. W. Osterwald)

127

Change of the most dramatic kind came in September, 1970 to **The Silverton** when light rain began to fall in the mountains around Silverton. The rain became heavy and was almost continuous for three days from September 4-6. A total of 4.19 inches fell on Silverton during the three-day deluge. High water in Mineral Creek roared into the lower portions of Silverton, knocked out the new sewage treatment plant, destroyed the Mineral Creek campground, and many local roads. The water supply system for Silverton was badly damaged and water covered the lower end of Silverton for about a day and a half.

Private property hardest hit by this flood was the D&RGW track to Silverton. From a point just south of Tacoma, north all the way to Silverton, parts of the track were either badly damaged or entirely destroyed. In some places the roadbed had to be completely rebuilt. Gauges for measuring the flow of water past Tacoma were washed away, as also happened in the floods of 1900, 1911, and 1927. Old timers say that the 1970 flood was worse than the 1927 flood, but not as disastrous as the 1911 deluge.

Fortunately, no bridges for the Silverton branch were destroyed, although small bridges over the tributary streams emptying into the Animas were badly clogged with debris. The U.S. Forest Service bridge at Cascade Creek was washed away, however. Hardest hit were sections of track between Tacoma and Tank Creek, and in the Cascade Creek area, at Tefft and at Elk Park. In most of these locations, sections of track were washed completely away from the roadbed. Rock slides were numerous. The D&RGW started repairs as soon as the water receded. This work continued until snow drove the repair crews out of the canyon, but by November, motor speeders ("pop cars") could run over all 45 miles of track. Spring came early to the San Juans in 1971, and most of the railroad was in excellent shape for opening day, May 29, 1971. Slow orders were in effect at some places for a few weeks until the new roadbed had settled and stabilized.

Durango escaped serious damage in this flood. The Animas valley just north of the city looked like a large lake for awhile, but this area is a natural reservoir for high water of the Animas River, and no extensive damage was done except to roads, bridges and water systems.

Other major narrow gauge railroad news in 1970 concerned the final abandonment of all but 64 miles of the D&RGW's line between Farmington, N.M. and Alamosa, Colo. The abandonment notice was first filed by the railroad in September, 1967. In August, 1968 the ICC recommended that the abandonment be permitted, and one year later the final approval was authorized by the ICC. Throughout most of this period, individuals, preservation societies, and some towns and cities in southwestern Colorado and northern New Mexico tried to fight the abandonment. It was not until February, 1969, when the legislatures of Colorado and New Mexico formed the Colorado and New Mexico Railroad Authorities, that any effective action was taken to save at least a portion of this route. A final passenger train was operated by the Rio Grande in November, 1968 from Durango to Alamosa for interested groups and for National Park Service representatives. In July, 1970 the two states, through their Railroad Authorities, purchased the line between Antonito, Colo. and Chama, New Mexico, and a large amount of equipment. This portion is presently leased to a concessionaire who operates the Cumbres & Toltec Scenic Railroad during the summer months. The other 110 miles of track have been dismantled, the rail and most rolling stock sold for scrap and some cars burned.

On Sept. 10, 1970, four days after the flood waters receeded, these photos were taken near Tacoma. The extensive damage to the roadbed and track are graphically illustrated. In the lower photo, the section of track was lifted off the roadbed and left in the stream channel.

(R. W. Osterwald)

SOMETHING NEW

A new and exciting era in the history of **The Silverton** began on May 23, 1981 when Mr. Charles E. Bradshaw, Jr., President of the Durango & Silverton Narrow Gauge Railroad, cut a red ribbon stretched across the track in front of the first double-headed passenger train to leave Durango in 19 years. On opening day over 600 passengers rode that first D&SNG train to Silverton in the familiar but newly painted and re-lettered Durango & Silverton coaches. During the the first six days of operation, 1022 more people rode the train than during the same six days of 1980. Enthusiastic tourists and rail fans filled 15-car double-headed trains during the first three days and on the fourth day an 11-car train carried people from all over the United States and from many foriegn countries. Similar increases in ridership have continued during the succeeding years.

Throughout the 1960s and 1970s the D&RGW attempted to find a suitable buyer for its isolated branch in the San Juans. Finally on March 25, 1981, the sale of **The Silverton** to Mr. Bradshaw of Orlando, Florida was completed after almost four years of planning and negotiation. He paid 2.2 million dollars in cash for this last remaining vestige of the once extensive D&RGW narrow gauge system. Included were 9 locomotives and all the structures, rolling stock and work equipment. Mr. Bradshaw is pledged to continue to operate, maintain and improve the line far beyond efforts of its former owner.

Amos Cordova, long-time depot agent for the Rio Grande, is Vice President and Treasurer and is in charge of station operations. James M. Mayer, also a long-time D&RGW employee and Trainmaster, was the first Vice President and superintendent of Maintainence and Operations for the D&SNG. George S. Connor, another former Rio Grande official, was the first Trainmaster, Road Foreman of Equipment and Director of Safety. Mr. Connor became Vice President and Superintendent after Mr. Mayer returned to the Rio Grande in May 1983.

Long before the purchase agreement was signed in July 1979, Mr. Bradshaw commissioned extensive engineering studies on the track, bridges and structures. It was found that by widening some rock cuts and strengthening some bridges, larger and heavier locomotives could operate safely. By August 1981, newly painted and refurbished engine 481 was the first K-36 engine to go beyond Rockwood in the 100-year history of the Silverton Branch. After its starring role in Durango's Centennial celebration, August 5, 1981, engine 481 first ran to Silverton August 7 and was placed in regular service on August 12.

During the first year of D&SNG operation, achievements were many. Double-headed trains, long a rarity on the road, frequently left the Durango depot. Much equipment, idle since 1968, was restored and returned to service. A 200-foot long car shop with 8400 square feet of work space was built on the site of the old one torn down by the Rio Grande. Although the new building looks much like its predecessor on the outside, it is completely equipped with modern machinery to restore, rebuild and build narrow gauge cars and equipment. The restoration to passenger service of dilapidated and seemingly derelict work equipment continued at a fast pace, several new open coaches were built from old standard gauge cattle cars, and two more engines have been rebuilt and placed in service.

Newly restored engine 497 steamed past the Needleton water tank in July 1984.

A Silverton–bound D&SNG train along the Animas River near Needleton Siding pulled by 478.

(Both photos by Kenneth T. Gustafson)

CENTENNIAL CELEBRATIONS

Anniversaries are always important occasions — and offer a chance to look backward at past history. On July 11, 1882 the Silverton Branch of the D&RG Railway was completed and opened for business. Thus Silverton was linked with "the outside world." No longer did rattling stage coaches and wagons lumber into town after an exhausting trip on the Wrightman toll road. One could ride to Durango in the style and comfort of a passenger coach — even heated in winter! Silverton's growth and survival depended upon the railroad a hundred years ago, just as it does today.

The 100th anniversary of the arrival of the first D&RG train in Durango was celebrated on August 5, 1981, when Colorado Governor Richard D. Lamm, D&SNG Railroad President Charles E. Bradshaw Jr., and a group of Durango community leaders and citizens rode a special train, pulled by engine 481, into Durango from the Iron Horse Resort north of town. A large and enthusiastic crowd enjoyed a picnic, parade and watched the ceremony of driving two silver spikes into a tie at the Durango depot. The spikes were deftly pounded into place by Gov. Lamm and by Alva F. Lyons, long-time D&RGW Conductor and Durango resident. Following the ceremony the spikes were immediately removed — one was given to the City of Durango and the other was auctioned off to the highest bidder, who turned out to be Charlie Bradshaw. He announced that the spike would remain in Durango and be on display at the depot. Bradshaw also pledged to preserve the railroad, its history and authenticity, so that people can continue to enjoy an unforgettable ride along the Animas for many years to come.

Another important anniversary was celebrated in 1982. The National Railway Historical Society held its National Convention in Denver from July 8-18, 1982 and as part of the convention activities, the society chartered a special excursion on the D&SNG July 11, 1982. Two trains loaded with convention delegates and their families stopped at Cascade Canyon wye for a brief ceremony to commemorate the 100th anniversary of the Silverton Branch. A simple monument of Colorado red granite commemorating the "Spirit of Colorado Mountain Railroading" was dedicated by officials of the NRHS and the D&SNG. The Silverton Gold Nugget Brass Band provided appropriate music and the trains carried a special D&S Railway Postal Station to cancel commemorative postal cachets. Other anniversary activities were planned by the Silverton Chamber of Commerce lasting 10 days, starting July 4, 1982. This was indeed an exciting year in the long and eventful history of **The Silverton!**

(Becky Osterwald)

Passengers on the two chartered trains gathered around the covered monument at the Cascade Canyon wye on July 11, 1982 and after brief introductions and remarks by several railroad and NRHS officials, Mr. Charles E. Bradshaw Jr., President of the D&SNG, unveiled the monument.   *(Becky Osterwald)*

Master of Ceremonies, Mr. Alexis McKinney, a retired D&RGW official, (left), and Mr. Bradshaw, (right) look at the monument after the unveiling.   *(D. B. Osterwald)*

THE RESTORATION OF ENGINE 480

It was late in the afternoon on a hot July 2, 1985, when the D&SNG roundhouse crew made the final check, put water in the tender, started a fire and carefully watched as steam pressure started to build in this rejuvenated relic of the 1920's. Several more days were then spent making adjustments and "fine-tuning" the iron horse's innards.

On July 9, the historic day finally arrived when engine 480 was ready for a trial run to Rockwood. Superintendent George Connor served as engineer and Assistant Trainmaster Dan McCall was fireman. Many of the roundhouse crew went along in caboose 0505. Stops were made along the route to adjust a squeaky lubricator. "It runs like a Cadillac when it doesn't squeak, but more like a Model T when it does," remarked Connor. He also added, "we expected it to be almost impossible (to restore engine 480) — and it was!"

At Rockwood, the engine was turned on the wye and the crew poured and squirted oil into every possible moving part before starting back to Durango. The train stopped at Hermosa for water and picked up a flat car. Few who saw that decrepit collection of rusty metal in 1981 believed the engine could be resurrected and returned to service. Engineers usually bestow feminine names on their engines, but perhaps the name "Lazarus" would be appropriate for engine 480!

If only this engine could tell of its past service! We do know it was built by Baldwin and purchased new by the D&RGW in 1925. What stories it might tell of engineers who pulled the whistle cord, of firemen who sweated to keep the firebox filled with coal, of the passenger, freight and excursion trains, of the accidents and of the time spent plowing snow in the Colorado mountains. These records would be lost to time were it not for photographers who captured a little of this history on film. Engine 480 was stationed at Salida, was often seen on Marshall Pass, at Gunnison, Garfield, Maysville and it helped dismantle the Valley Line between Mears Junction and Hooper, Colo. in 1951. It also knew Durango, Chama, Cumbres Pass, and Farmington, N.M. quite well — but never reached Silverton because the cuts were too narrow and the bridges needed to be strengthened to handle K-36 engines.

According to Jackson C. Thode, retired D&RGW official and railroad historian, engine 480 was used intermittently until 1964. It was retired from service by the D&RGW on May 31, 1964 and stored in the Alamosa roundhouse until about 1969. From 1969 until 1981, engine 480 sat idle outside the Alamosa shops while rust and vandalism reduced it to an inoperable mass of metal parts. When purchased by the D&SNG in 1981, engines 480, 493 and 498 had to be moved from Alamosa to Durango. It's not every day one sees a locomotive on the Main Street of Alamosa, or coming out of the highway snowshed on Wolf Creek Pass, but during May 1981 such an event occurred three times! Because there are no longer rails between Chama, N.M. and Durango, the only way for these engines to be returned to Durango was by transporting them on a low-boy truck. Weicker Moving and Storage Co. of Pueblo, was in charge of all moving operations.

Engines 493 and 498 had been stored in the Alamosa roundhouse and were in better shape. In order to load them onto a truck, the rails in front of the roundhouse were cut and removed. Then a sloping pit was dug so that a 12-wheel low-boy trailer could back up to the roundhouse, matching the rails, which had been attached to the bed of the truck, with those still in place at the roundhouse entrance. (A very tricky maneuver!) After lining up the rails, each engine was winched onto the bed of the truck. An 8-wheel dolly was added between the tractor and trailer, and a 4-wheel dolly to the rear of the trailer to distribute the estimated 75- to 80-ton load for the trip to Durango.

When restoration of 480 started, it was found that many parts were missing. Steve Jackson, Roundhouse Foreman, remarked, "someone did us a big favor — we didn't have to take the engine apart." New grates, firebox door, Johnson bar, throttle parts and the smoke box interior were cast. New wiring, steam and air lines, injectors, boiler check valves, pilot, fountain and snifter valves were also made. Many other parts needed extensive repairs, such as the lubricators. The engine was stripped, sandblasted and inspected, the flues and superheater unit were pulled and inspected, and after passing hydro-tests, parts were fabricated as needed. The running gear was re-bushed. A bell and whistle were found in a boxcar of parts left by the Rio Grande.

Engine 480 pulled its first revenue train, No. 265, the afternoon **Cascade Canyon** from Durango to Cascade Canyon wye on July 13, 1985. At Rockwood the balky lubricator had to be adjusted again and a few loose bolts tightened. The trip ran late because it was found the clearances between the engine and tender were too close on the tight curves, so slow running was in order. Engineer Bill Huffman remarked, "It's a good engine. I didn't have to get above the second throttle notch." Fireman Ray Loose said it, "rides smooth and fires easy." The next morning the needed adjustments were made and train No. 265 was called, with shiny and bright engine 480. On July 15, 1985, the 480 pulled its first train to Silverton, the 7:30 AM **San Juan Express**, train No. 115.

The 480's have the reputation among railroaders of being the best narrow gauge steam engines owned by the D&RGW, and one of the most efficient designs of either gauge. Engine 480 is living up to that reputation.

D&RGW engine 480 leaving Chama, N.M. with a 44-car westboard freight extra on Sept. 1, 1940. The consist included a narrow-gauge refrigerator car. Note that the tender has the old style lettering and not the later style "Flying Rio Grande." (Photo courtesy R. H. Kindig)

135

D&RGW engine 480, double-headed with 496, stopped near Romeo, Colo. May 31, 1958. (Photo courtesy R. H. Kindig)

K-36 engine 480 was stored outside and in order to load it onto the truck, a pit was dug, rails cut and the truck backed into the pit for loading. When the winch first started to pull 480, one could hear and see rust pop off the drivers, and dead tumbleweeds under the engine were crushed as the engine was very slowly moved onto the truck. As one retired railroader commented while watching the loading, "There is nothing deader than a dead locomotive."

After an over night stop at South Fork, the tractor-trailer rig "Ol' Blue," owned by Dick Arfsten of Henderson, Colorado, started toward Wolf Creek Pass at 6:30 A.M. on May 4, 1981 with 480 coming along for the ride. The snowshed was reached at 7:30 A.M. and the summit about 8 A.M. The descent was even slower! (D. B. Osterwald)

About 2:30 P.M. the same day, 480 finally arrived in Durango. A broken wheel on "Ol' Blue" at the top of Yellowjacket Pass slowed the arrival by several hours. This picture was taken just before the truck was backed into another sloping pit dug along the west side of the roundhouse. After matching the rails and removing the anchoring chains from the engine, 480 slowly was rolled from the truck onto the rails by releasing the winch cable on "Ol' Blue". Engine 480 had come back to Durango!
(F. W. Osterwald)

Train No. 265 (engine 480) meeting train No. 462 (engine 481) at Home Ranch Siding, July 14, 1985. (F. W. Osterwald)

*Engine 480 pulled train 115, the **San Juan Express**, to Silverton for the first time on July 15, 1985. After just three runs, the smokebox no longer looked bright and shiny, as the train turned at the Silverton wye.* (Photo courtesy George Chapman)

TRAGEDY STRIKES THE NARROW GAUGE

Problems are nothing new to railroaders on the narrow gauge. During the winter, tracks often were blocked by huge snowdrifts and avalanches. Mud slides, broken or kinked rails, washouts and rocks on the tracks caused many delays and derailments (to call them "wrecks" was a firing offense on the Rio Grande narrow gauge). Strangely enough, however, few injuries or deaths resulted from these events.

In about 1920, general car foreman Monte Ballough recorded this minor derailment at the Durango roundhouse. Engine 281, a Baldwin C-16, was standing on a yard track under steam. A leaky throttle caused 281 to slowly "walk" into the turntable pit. This engine, built in 1882, was finally retired in 1926. (Collection of M. B. Palmer)

Another more serious accident occurred in July 1951 when engine 473, pulling a freight from Silverton to Durango with 900 tons of silver ore and concentrates, encountered a sun-kink in the track near the east switch at Needleton. The engine and tender got a bath in the Animas River, but all the cars stayed on the rails. No one was injured. (Collection of Edna Sanborn)

Engine 473 is no stranger to trucks. In June 1974, a truck pacing the train on a road paralleling the track a few miles north of Durango, suddenly swerved into the engine. A new injector (the large bronze casting that forces water into the boiler from the tender) and a few other items had to be replaced after the engine returned to Durango under its own power.

Several years ago, the engine was broadsided by a truck at a grade crossing in Durango. Needless to say, the truck was more damaged than the engine.

If 473 had not suffered enough aches and pains from trucks in the past, it suffered even more on June 25, 1987. The engine was steamed up and fully loaded with coal on the ready track beside the Durango roundhouse, waiting to depart for Silverton. An 18-wheel truck loaded with almost 24 tons of loose potatoes lost its brakes near the top of Hesperus Hill, 14 miles west of Durango on U.S. 160. The truck careened down the canyon, went through the intersection of U.S. 160 and U.S.550 (fortunately with a green light!!), hit the embankment east of the intersection where it became airborne and plowed through a chain-link fence before crunching to a stop against the fireman's side of 473.

D&SNG hostlers John Hood and Gilbert Sanchez fortunately saw the truck flying toward them and jumped to safety. Remarkably, the trucker, Neal Fox of Colorado Springs, suffered only a broken leg and ankle but it took nearly an hour to free him from the wreckage.

The engine was knocked 11 feet off the track by the impact. Once again, 473 needed a new injector. The steel-plated cab floor was badly buckled and the cab and coal deck on the tender had to be replaced as did many feet of pipes and air lines. After three weeks of intensive repairs, a trial run on July 17 and several days of adjustments and fine-tuning, 473 was back in regular service.

The scene at the roundhouse shortly after Durango firemen arrived. Fortunately the truck missed the firebox and boiler or a steam explosion and fire could have resulted. *(Paul Conner photo©)*

After the mangled truck was pulled away from 473, the damage to both vehicles is apparent. The truck was totaled and 473 required $50,000 to $60,000 to repair.
(Paul Connor photo©)

The 10-stall Durango roundhouse was built in 1881 and remained essentially the same until June 1965 when the roof and doorways of stalls 4, 5, and 6 (numbered from east to west) were raised so 480 and 490 series engines could be moved all the way into the building. The rear walls of these stalls were also moved back because these engines are longer than the ones used in 1881.

After the track from Alamosa was abandoned, the four western stalls, numbers 7, 8, 9, and 10 were removed in early 1971 and a new roof was installed on the remaining six. The three stalls on the east beside the foreman's office were converted into a machine shop. After the D&SNG bought the railroad, the four missing stalls were replaced in 1985.

This photo, taken during the late 1930s, shows the original roundhouse and the 65-foot turntable that was moved from Alamosa in 1924 to replace a 50-foot one.
(Denver Public Library, Western History Department)

FIRE DESTROYS THE DURANGO ROUNDHOUSE

In the early morning of February 10, 1989 roaring flames had all but destroyed the 108-year old Durango roundhouse. All six engines were inside.

(Paul Connor photo©)

A night security guard discovered fire in the southeastern corner of the roundhouse machine shop, behind a metal-treating kiln. Investigators believe the fire started from a piece of hot metal thrown off from some grinding done on Thursday afternoon. The hot metal fragment apparently lodged in the fibreboard wall behind the kiln. Flames spread rapidly and soon engulfed the entire building. All six operable engines were in the roundhouse and at first it was feared all were damaged beyond repair. Daylight brought hope and some optimism as the smoldering embers and hot metal cooled.

Temperatures near the roof of the roundhouse were estimated to have reached 2500° to 3000° F. When the roof collapsed, heavy timbers and the steel smoke jacks fell on the engines, causing extensive damage to headlights, smoke boxes wiring and piping. In addition to the burning of heavy roof timbers, wooden parts of the cabs also burned. Because rising heat from the burning roof created a strong draft, cold air from outside was drawn in near the floor, probably filling the work pits under the engines. This prevented much damage below the running boards, except for deformed brass bushings in the running gear. The intense heat burned all the paint off the engines, so quick repainting became a top priority on the least damaged engines. The machine shop was totally destroyed as were many spare parts that are no longer available. But the skilled and dedicated roundhouse crew, working largely in the open, made the necessary parts.

One week later, all the debris and destroyed machinery had been cleaned out and a temporary machine shop built along the still standing west wall of the roundhouse. Some machine tools were borrowed, others were purchased second-hand, and new machines continue to arrive. Temporary electric power

*Engine 480 was in stall 6 near the western fire
wall of the roundhouse.*

*Engine 497 in stall 5 was the least damaged of
the six.*

was installed in the open-air roundhouse and a crew of 16 men went back to work
on the engines they love. Fortunately the winter weather turned mild and
working outside was not too large a problem.

The photographs at the top of this page and pages 144–145 were taken by Eric
Nelson of Lafayette, Colo. two days after the fire. They dramatically illustrate
the depressing sight that greeted heartsick D&S employees and everyone else in
Durango. The pictures are arranged in the same order in which the engines stood
in the roundhouse.

Engine 480 was badly damaged because heat radiated back from the firewall
to the engine. The roof and smoke jack collapsed and all but buried the engine—
only the damaged headlight appeared through the rubble.

Engine 497, standing next to 480, was the least damaged and the first one
crews attempted to move from the roundhouse; 497 refused to move. Both
cylinders were completely full of ice from all the water used to douse the fire and
protect the engines. The solution: small fires were built under each cylinder to
melt the ice! Then the engine was washed with a high pressure hose, moved to
the car shop and painted. It needed some cab repairs and some new parts and
gauges. A new tender tank was already on order.

In stall 4 engine 481 was up on blocks for extensive maintenance so it was
the last to be moved. The front of engine 478 in stall 3 was clearly recognizable
as a locomotive and was little damaged. Repairs were started immediately and
it was ready on opening day.

Engines 481 (left) and 478 (right) on the morning of February 12, 1989.

(Eric Nelson)

Two views of the machine shop along the north wall of the roundhouse the day after the fire. The strange shapes draped around the work area are electrical conduits left suspended when the roof collapsed. Among the identifiable objects in the debris are a drill press, a vertical mill, several copper hydraulic lines, some gauges and part of a lathe.

(Paul Connor photos©)

Engines 476 (left) and 473 (right). The 473 in stall 1 suffered the worst damage because it was closest to the source of the fire and because the tender was fully loaded with coal which burned. The steam dome was damaged and the cab totally destroyed. Poor number 473 was completely overhauled in 1988 and was ready to be fired up with a boiler half full of water. But D&SNG officials are confident that this invincible engine will be back in service by mid-summer. (Eric Nelson)

eyond the rubble at the rear of the roundhouse, engine 476 sits forlornly and forsaken in stall on February 11, 1989. This engine was first to be returned to service. It made a successful ial run on April 13 to Cascade Wye, pulling seven empty coaches. As it left Durango it passed nder crossed ladders of Durango Fire Department equipment, a fitting tribute of the nportance of the D&SNG to Durango and southwestern Colorado. (Paul Connor photo©)

WORK IN THE OPEN AIR ROUNDHOUSE

By April 7, 1989 a great deal of optimism had returned to Durango and work "in" the roundhouse continued at a feverish pace. George Connor, Vice President and Superintendent of the D&SNG, said that some good would result from the fire because the old roundhouse really was not adequate to service the growing list of operable engines. Rebuilding the roundhouse will start during the summer. The new design will follow the original roundhouse as closely as possible. The original brick walls that are still standing probably will remain. The D&SNG Railroad is back on the track!

Remains of the northeastern corner of the roundhouse and the foreman's office, April 7, 1989. *(F. W. Osterwald)*

This view graphically illustrates how much was accomplished in less than two months time. From left to right are engines 481, newly painted 478, 497 and 476 (behind the Pettibone machine) and 480. *(F. W. Osterwald)*

Close-up of engine 481 on April 7, 1989. At the time of the fire, 481 had no boiler jacket, lagging or flues and both the smoke-box front and the firebox doors were open so heat from the fire went completely through the engine. Workers were still replacing the boiler jacket, external fitting and repairing the smoke-box. Engine 478 looked as if it had just some from the American Locomotive Co. factory! (F. W. Osterwald)

Along the northeastern wall of the "roundhouse", newly refurbished main and side-rods for engine 480 were laid out on the cement floor which shows no signs of the fire. New brass bushings for the rods were turned on a lathe in the plastic-and-plywood temporary machine shop. (F. W. Osterwald)

BACK ON TRACK

The annual opening day on the narrow gauge is always a special time, but the festivities for the May 5–6, 1989 opening were even more notable because of the Durango roundhouse fire in February. It was with a great sense of relief and gratitude to all employees of the Durango & Silverton Narrow Gauge Railroad that the Durango Chamber of Commerce and other tourism organizations planned "Full Steam Ahead Days" to welcome the return of **The Silverton**.

Friday's noontime activities, held at the corner of Fifth Street and Main Avenue, included the usual welcoming speeches, a Fly-By of Colorado Air National Guard jets, bands, Indian dancers and singing by Durango grade-schoolers. At a dinner that evening D&S Vice President Amos Cordova spoke of the problems and accomplishments of the past three months.

One highlight of these festivities was the introduction by Master of Ceremonies, C. W. McCall, of long-time D&RGW conductor of **The Silverton**, Alva Lyons. Lyons, who is 92 years young, worked for the Rio Grande for 51 years and was largely responsible for the campaign to save the Silverton Branch from abandonment. Following his introduction he gave a long, healthy and very energetic "All l l l Aboaarrrrd".

There were so many reservations for opening day that two sections of train 461 left the Durango depot 15 minutes apart. The first section, pulled by shiny engine 476 carrying green flags, steamed northward at 8:30 A.M. as hundreds of well-wishers lined the streets to wave and take pictures. The second section was pulled by engine 497 which also looked like it had just come from the factory.

The extremely mild weather through March and April made it possible for the D&S roundhouse crew to complete repairs on the engines, but it also meant that snow in the mountains melted much too soon. On the way to Silverton a spark from one of the engines started a small forest fire near Cascade. Perhaps everyone has heard the word "fire" enough for one year.

Silverton, Colorado on May 6, 1989, after the second section of train 461, pulled by 497 arrived. Green marker flags on engine 476 indicated that a second section was following. Engine 476 lost one of its markers before reaching Hermosa.   *(Ren Osterwald)*

REFERENCES

GEOLOGY

Atwood, W. W., and Mather, K. F., 1932, Physiography and Quaternary Geology of the San Juan Mountains, Colorado: U.S. Geol. Survey Prof. Paper 166.

Baars, D. L., and Knight, R. L., 1957, Pre-Pennsylvanian Stratigraphy of the San Juan Mountains and Four Corners Area in New Mexico Geol. Soc. Guidebook, 8th Field Conf., Southwestern San Juan Mountains, Colorado, page 108-131.

Burbank, W. S., Eckel, E. B., and Varnes, D. J., 1947, The San Juan region (Colorado): Colorado Mineral Resources Board Bull., page 396-446.

Canfield, John C., 1893, Mines and Mining Men of Colorado: Denver, Colo.

Cross, Whitman, Howe, Ernest, and Ransome, F. L., 1905, Description of the Silverton Quadrangle, Colorado: U.S. Geol. Survey, Geol. Atlas, Folio 120.

Cross, Whitman, Howe, Ernest, Irving, J. D., and Emmons, W. H., 1905, Description of the Needle Mountains Quadrangle, Colorado: U.S. Geol. Survey Geol. Atlas, Folio 131.

Cross, Whitman, and Hole, Allen D., 1910, Description of the Engineer Mountain Quadrangle, Colorado: U.S. Geol. Survey Geol. Atlas, Folio 171.

Endlich, F. M., 1876, Report [on the San Juan district, Colorado]: U.S. Geol. and Geog. Survey Terr. (Hayden), Ann. Rept. 8, page 181-240.

George, R. D., 1920, Mineral Waters of Colorado: Colo. Geol. Survey Bull. 11.

Henderson, C. W., 1926, Mining in Colorado, a History of Discovery, Development, and Production: U.S. Geol. Survey, Prof. Paper 138.

Kelley, Vincent C., 1957, General Geology and Tectonics of the Western San Juan Mountains, Colorado in New Mexico Geol. Soc. Guidebook, 8th Field Conf., Southwestern San Juan Mountains, Colorado, page 154-162.

Kelley, Vincent C., 1957, Vein and Fault Systems of the Western San Juan Mountains Mineral Belt, Colorado in New Mexico Geol. Soc. Guidebook, 8th Field Conf., Southwestern San Juan Mountains, Colorado, page 173-176.

Kilgore, Lee W., 1955, Geology of the Durango Area, La Plata County, Colorado in Four Corners Geological Society Guidebook, No. 1, page 118-124.

Kottlowski, Frank E., 1957, Mesozoic Strata Flanking the Southwestern San Juan Mountains, Colo. and New Mexico in New Mexico Geol. Soc. Guidebook, 8th Field Conf., Southwestern San Juan Mountains, Colorado, page 138-153.

Larsen, Esper S., Jr., and Cross, Whitman, 1956, Geology and Petrology of the San Juan Region, Southwestern Colorado: U.S. Geol. Survey, Prof. Paper 258.

Lochman-Balk, Christina, 1956, The Cambrian of the Rocky Mountains and Southwest Deserts of the United States and Adjoining Sonora Province, Mexico: International Geological Congress part II, Australia, America, page 562-565.

Mather, Kirtley F., 1957, Geomorphology of The San Juan Mountains in New Mexico Geol. Soc. Guidebook, 8th Field Conf., Southwestern San Juan Mountains, Colorado, page 102-108.

Ransome, F. L., 1901, A Report on the Economic Geology of the Silverton Quadrangle, Colorado: U.S. Geol. Survey, Bull. 182.

Silver, Caswell, 1957, Silverton to Durango via Railroad in New Mexico Geol. Soc. Guidebook, 8th Field Conf., Southwestern San Juan Mountains, Colorado, page 75-90.

Stokes, Wm. Lee, and Varnes, David J., 1955, Glossary of Selected Geologic Terms: Colorado Scientific Soc. Proc., vol. 16.

Tewksbury, B. J., 1985, Revised interpretation of the ages of allochthonous rocks of the Uncompahgre Formation, Needle Mountains, Colo.; Geol. Soc. America Bull. v. 96, p. 224-232.

Varnes, David J., 1963, Geology and Ore Deposits of the South Silverton Mining Area, San Juan County, Colorado: U.S. Geol. Survey, Prof. Paper 378-A.

Wengerd, Sherman A., and Baars, Donald L., 1957, Durango to Silverton Road Log in New Mexico Geol. Soc. Guidebook, 8th Field Conf., Southwestern San Juan Mountains, Colo. page 39-51.

Wengerd, Sherman, A., 1957, Permo-Pennsylvania Strata of the Western San Juan Mountains, Colorado in New Mexico Geol. Soc. Guidebook, 8th Field Conf., Southwestern San Juan Mountains, Colorado, page 131-138.

Zapp, A. D., 1949, Geology and Coal Resources of the Durango Area, La Plata and Montezuma Counties, Colorado: U.S. Geol. Survey Oil and Gas Inv., Prelim. Map 109.

HISTORY

Ayers, Mary C., 1951, Howardsville in the San Juan: The Colo. Mag., Vol. XXXVIII, No. 4.

Bender, Norman J., 1964, History of The Durango Area in Four Corners Geological Soc., Durango-Silverton Guidebook, page 18-29.

Darley, George M., 1899, Pioneering in the San Juan: Chicago, Ill.

Hall, Frank, 1895, History of the State of Colorado: Chicago, 4 vol.

Ingersoll, Ernest, 1882, Silvery San Juan: Harpers, Vol. LXIV, No. 383, page 689-704.

Ingersoll, Ernest, 1885, The Crest of the Continent: R. R. Donnelley, Chicago, Ill.

Logan, Kenneth T., 1962, The History of La Plata County: The Encyclopedia of Colorado, Colo. Historical Assoc., page 278-282.

Marshall, John B., 1962, History of San Juan County: The Encyclopedia of Colorado, Colorado Historical Assoc., page 311-316.

Mathews, Ruth Estelle, 1940, A Study of Colorado Place Names: Unpub. M. A. Thesis, Stanford U., Palo Alto, Calif.

Newhall, Beaumont, and Edkins, Diana E., 1974, William H. Jackson: Morgan and Morgan, Amon Carter Museum, Ft. Worth, Texas, 158 pages.

Olsen, Mary Ann, 1962, The Silverton Story, Bearber Printing Co., Cortez, Colo. 28 pages.

Pinkert, Leta, 1964, True Stories of Early Days in the San Juan Basin: Hustler Press, Inc., Farmington, N.M., 38 pages.

Sarah Platt Decker Chapter, N. S. D. A. R., 1942, 1946, 1952, 1961, Pioneers of the San Juan Country: Vol. I and II, Out West Printing Co., Vol. III, Durango Printing Co., Vol. IV, Big Mountain Press.

Silver, Caswell, 1957, History and Folklore of the San Juan Region **in** New Mexico Geol. Soc. Guidebook, 8th Field Conf., Southwestern San Juan Mountains, Colorado, page 222-234.

Thompson, Ian, 1964, The Silverton Country. A Historical Sketch: Four Corners Geol. Soc., Durango-Silverton Guidebook, page 1-5.

RAILROADS

Along the Narrow Gauge, 1964, U.S. Forest Service Pamphlet.

Anonymous, 1883, Official Railway Guide to Colorado, the East and West: Reprinted 1978 by Mobile Post Office Society, Omaha, Neb., 120 pages.

Athearn, Robert G., 1962, Rebel in the Rockies: Yale U. Press, New Haven, Conn., 395 pages.

Beebe, Lucius, and Clegg, Charles, 1958, Narrow Gauge in the Rockies: Howell-North, Berkeley, Calif., 224 pages.

Beebe, Lucius, and Clegg, Charles, 1962, Rio Grande, Mainline of the Rockies: Howell-North, Berkeley, Calif., 380 pages.

Carter, Kenneth E., 1964, The Narrow Gauge Lines: Four Corners Geol. Soc., Durango-Silverton Guidebook, page 7-17.

Chappell, Gordon S., 1971, Logging Along the Denver & Rio Grande: Colorado Railroad Museum, Golden, Colo., 190 pages.

Choda, Kelly, 1956, Thirty Pound Rails: The Filter Press, Aurora, Colorado, 46 pages.

Crum, Josie, M., not dated, The D&RG in The San Juan, pamphlet, 32 pages.

Crum, Josie, M., 1960, Three Little Lines: Durango Herald News, Durango, Colo., 71 pages.

Crum, Josie, M., 1956, Rails Among Peaks, The D&RG in the San Juan Mountains: Reprinted from Railway and Locomotive Hist. Soc. Bull. No. 76.

Crum, Josie Moore, 1961, The Rio Grande Southern Railroad, Hamilton Press, Inc., Durango, Colo., 431 pages.

Denver and Rio Grande Railroad records and photographs from 1871 to the present: Library, State Historical Society of Colorado.

Ghost Town and Calico Railway, 1953, Ghost Town, California, pamphlet, 59 pages.

Hauck, Cornelius W., and Richardson, Robert W., 1963, Steam in the Rockies, a Denver and Rio Grande Roster: Colorado Railroad Museum, Golden, Colo. 32 pages.

Hungerford, John B., 1955, Narrow Gauge to Silverton: Hungerford Press, Reseda, California, 36 pages.

Hunt, Louie, 1955, The Silverton Train: Leucadia, Calif.

Iron Horse News, compiled and edited by Robert W. Richardson, Colorado Railroad Museum, Golden, Colo., issues from 1951-1982.

LeMassena, R. A., 1964, Colorado's Mountain Railroads, Vol. III: Smoking Stack Press, Golden, Colorado.

LeMassena, Robert A., 1974, Rio Grande to the Pacific: Sundance Ltd., Denver, Colo., 416 pages.

Locomotives of the Rio Grande, 1980, Colorado Railroad Museum, Golden, Colo., 96 pages.

McCoy, Dell and Collman, Russ, 1971: The Rio Grande Pictorial 1871-1971, Sundance, Ltd., Denver, Colo., 216 pages.

McKinney, Alexis, 1979, The Silverton's three private cars: "Legends on Rails", **in** Colorado Rail Annual No. 14, Colorado Railroad Museum, Golden, Colo., page 9-23.

Ormes, Robert M., 1963, Railroads and the Rockies: Sage Books, Denver, Colorado, 406 pages.

The Silverton and "Rio Grande-land" **in** Colorado Annual, 1963: Colorado Railroad Museum, Golden, Colorado, 15 pages.

Thode, Jackson C., 1971, A Century of Passenger Trains, **in** The 1970 Denver Westerners Brand Book, The Westerners, Denver, Colo. pages 83-253.

To Silverton in Snow, **in** Colorado Annual, 1964: Colorado Railroad Museum, Golden, Colorado, 15 pages.

NATURE

Baerg, Harry J., 1955, How to Know the Western Trees: Wm. C. Brown Company, Dubuque, Iowa, 170 pages.

Craighead, John J., Craighead, Frank C., Jr., and Davis, Ray J., 1963, A Field Guide to Rocky Mountain Wildflowers: Houghton Mifflin Co., Boston, Mass., 277 pages.

Roberts, Harold and Roberts, Rhoda, 1959, Colorado Wild Flowers: Denver Museum of Natural History, Museum Pictorial No. 8, 63 pages.

Roberts, Rhoda N., and Nelson, Ruth Ashton, 1957, Mountain Wild Flowers of Colorado: Denver Museum of Natural History, Museum Pictorial No. 13, 64 pages.

Pesman, Walter M., 1948, Meet the Natives: Denver, Colo., 217 pages.

Peterson, Roger Tory, 1941, A Field Guide to Western Birds: Houghton Mifflin Co., Boston, Mass., 240 pages.

U.S. Dept. Agriculture, 1949, Trees, The Yearbook of Agriculture.

Weber, William A., 1961, Handbook of Plants of the Colorado Front Range: U. of Colo. Press, 232 pages.

Zim, Herbert S., 1964, The Rocky Mountains: Golden Press, New York, 160 pages.

NEWSPAPERS

Denver Post

Denver Republican

Denver Tribune

Durango Herald

Durango Daily Herald

Durango Record

La Plata Miner, Silverton, Colorado

Ouray Times

The Southwest, Animas City, Colorado

SOURCES FOR GUIDE MAPS

The geologic maps were compiled from the following maps and supplemented with personal field work:

U.S. Geological Survey, Folios Nos. 120, 131, 171.

U.S. Geological Survey Prof. Paper 258, plate I.

U.S. Geological Survey Prof. Paper 378-A, plate I.

Four Corners Geological Society, Durango-Silverton Guidebook, 1964, pages 67-71.

U.S. Geological Survey, Oil & Gas Inv., Prelim. Map 109.

EQUIPMENT ROSTER

LOCOMOTIVES

In Service	Year Built	Year Rebuilt
473	1923	D&SNG 1989
476	1923	D&SNG 1989
478	1923	D&SNG 1989
480	1925	D&SNG 1985, 1989
481	1925	D&SNG 1981, 1989
497	1902	D&RGW 1930
		D&SNG 1984, 1989

Not In Service	Year Built	Year Rebuilt
42	1887	Magic Mtn. 1958
(Ex-D&RG 420; Ex-RGS 42)		
493	1902	D&RGW 1928
498	1902	D&RGW 1930
499	1902	D&RGW 1930

PASSENGER AND SPECIAL-USE EQUIPMENT ON D&SNG ROSTER, MAY 1986

Car Number	Present Name	Present Use	Original Use	Year Built	Year Rebuilt	Use After Rebuilt
64	Baggage-Concession	Concessions	Mail-baggage No. 64	D&RG 1889	D&SNG 1984	Concession
126	Concession	Concessions	Baggage No. 27	D&RG 1883	D&RGW 1939	Baggage
					D&RGW 1963	Snack-bar car
					D&RGW 1979	Coach
					D&SNG 1982	Concession
212	Concession	Concessions	Coach No. 20	D&RG 1879	D&RG 1887	Coach-baggage No. 215
					D&RGW 1942	Coach-baggage No. 212
					D&RGW 1964	Snack-bar car
					D&RGW 1979	Coach
					D&SNG 1982	Snack-bar car
					D&SNG 1986	Concession
213	Home Ranch	Car for the Handicapped	Passenger-baggage	D&SNG 1983		
257	Bell	Coach	Coach No. 43	Jackson & Sharp 1880	D&RG 1886	Coach
					RGS 1891	Coach
					RGS 1920's	Passenger-baggage
					D&SNG 1986	Coach
270	Pinkerton	Coach	Coach No. 46	Jackson & Sharp 1880	D&RGW 1924	Kitchen-diner outfit car
					D&SNG 1982	Coach
291	King Mine	Coach	Coach No. 67	Jackson & Sharp 1881	D&RGW 1924	Non-revenue work svc.
					D&SNG 1984	Coach
311	McPhee	Coach	Coach No. 87	Jackson & Sharp 1881	D&SNG 1984	
312	Silverton	Coach	Coach No. 312	D&RG 1887	D&RGW 1937	First-class coach
					D&RGW 1957	Coach
					D&RGW 1979	Coach
319	Needleton	Coach	Coach No. 95	Jackson & Sharp 1882	D&RGW 1937	First-class coach
					D&RGW 1957	Coach
					D&RGW 1978	Coach
323	Animas City	Coach	Coach No. 323	D&RG 1887	D&RGW 1937	First-class coach
					D&RGW 1957	Coach
					D&RGW 1978	Coach
327	Durango	Coach	Coach No. 327?	D&RG 1887	D&RGW 1937	First-class coach
					D&RGW 1957	Coach
					D&RGW 1978	Coach
330	Cascade	Coach	Coach	D&RGW 1963		
331	Trimble	Coach	Coach	D&RGW 1963		
332	La Plata	Coach	Coach	D&RGW 1964		
333	Tacoma	Coach	Coach	D&RGW 1964		
334	Hermosa	Coach	Coach	D&RGW 1964		
335	Elk Park	Coach	Coach	D&RGW 1964		
336	Rockwood	Coach	Coach	D&RGW 1964		
337	San Juan	Coach	Coach	D&RGW 1964		
566	Concession	Concessions	Mail No. 14	D&RG 1882	D&RG ca. 1888	Excursion car
					D&RG 1914	B&B Foreman coach-outfit car
					D&SNG 1982	Concession
630	Hunt	Coach	Coach	D&SNG 1984		
631	North Star	Coach	Coach	D&SNG 1985		
632	Tefft	Coach	Coach	D&SNG 1986		

OPEN OBSERVATION CARS

400	—	Open Observation	S.G. Boxcar 67191	Pullman 1916	D&RGW 1953	N.G. Pipe Car 9609
					D&RGW 1963	
401	—	Open Observation	S.G. Boxcar 66665	Pullman 1916	D&RGW 1953	N.G. Pipe Car 9611
					D&RGW 1963	

402. . . . — . . . . Open . . . . S.G. Boxcar. . . . Pullman 1916. . . . D&RGW 1953 . . . . . N.G. Pipe Car 9605
                        Observation   66271   D&RGW 1963

403. . . . — . . . . Open . . . . S.G. Boxcar. . . . Pullman 1916. . . . D&RGW 1953 . . . . . N.G. Pipe Car 9606
                        Observation   D&RGW 1964

404. . . . — . . . . Open . . . . S.G. Boxcar. . . . Pullman 1916. . . . D&RGW 1953 . . . . . N.G. Pipe Car 9600
                        Observation   D&RGW 1964

405. . . . — . . . . Open . . . . S.G. Boxcar. . . . Pullman 1916. . . . D&RGW 1953 . . . . . N.G. Pipe Car 9601
                        Observation   D&RGW 1964

406. . . . — . . . . Open . . . . S.G. Stk. Car. . . 1937 . . . . D&SNG 1985 . . . . .
                        Observation

407. . . . — . . . . Open . . . . S.G. Stk. Car. . . 1937 . . . . D&SNG 1985 . . . . .
                        Observation

408. . . . — . . . . Open . . . . S.G. Stk. Car. . . 1937 . . . . D&SNG 1985-86 . . .
                        Observation

409. . . . — . . . . Open . . . . S.G. Stk. Car. . . 1937 . . . . D&SNG 1985-86 . . .
                        Observation

411. . . . — . . . . Open . . . . S.G. Boxcar. . . Pullman 1916. . . . D&RGW 1953? . . . . N.G. Pipe Car 9603
                        Observation   D&SNG 1982   Partial Rebuild to 405
                                                       D&SNG 1985

412. . . . — . . . . Open . . . . S.G. Boxcar. . . Pullman 1916. . . . D&RGW 1953? . . . . N.G. Pipe Car 9608
                        Observation   D&SNG 1982   Partial Rebuild to 406
                                                       D&SNG 1985-86

413. . . . — . . . . Open . . . . S.G. Stk. Car. . . 1937 . . . . D&SNG 1983 . . . . .
                        Observation

414. . . . — . . . . Open . . . . S.G. Stk. Car. . . 1937 . . . . D&SNG 1984 . . . . .
                        Observation

415. . . . — . . . . Open . . . . S.G. Stk. Car. . . 1937 . . . . D&SNG 1984 . . . . .
                        Observation

416. . . . — . . . . Open . . . . S.G. Stk. Car. . . 1937 . . . . D&SNG 1989 . . . . .
                        Observation

SPECIAL CARS

350. . . . Alamosa . . . . . . Parlor Car . . . . Chaircar . . . . . . Jackson & . . . . . . D&RG 1919. . . . . . . Office-living car
                              No. 25   Sharp 1880   D&RGW 1924   Parlor-smoker car
                                                        D&RGW 1937   Parlor-buffet car
                                                        D&RGW 1957   Coach
                                                        D&RGW 1978   Coach
                                                        D&SNG 1981   Parlor-car

B-2 . . . . Cinco Animas . . Private Car. . . . Emigrant . . . . . D&RG 1883. . . . . D&RG 1909. . . . . . . Paycar "F"
                           for Charter   Sleeper No. 103   D&RG 1917   Business car B-2
                                                        Cinco Animas
                                                        Corp. 1963   Private observation car

B-3 . . . . Nomad. . . . . . . Private Car. . . . Chaircar . . . . . Billmeyer & . . . . D&RG 1886. . . . . . . Business car "N"
                              No. 16   Small 1878   D&RG 1917   Officer's sleeping car
                                                        Private 1957   Private observation car
                                                        D&SNG 1987   Private observation car

3681 . . . Railcamp Car . . Avail. for . . . . . Narrow-gauge . . 1903 or 1904 . . . . D&RGW 1924 . . . . .
                              Charter   Boxcar 3681   D&SNG 1984

Cars Not In Service

460 . . . . Coach . . . . Emigrant- . . . . . D&RG 1886. . . . . D&RG 1903. . . . . . . Construction outfit car
                              Sleeper   D&RG 1914. . . . . . . Kitchen-diner outfit car
                                                        D&RGW 1923 . . . . Work train outfit car
                                                        BHC 1957 . . . . Coach

B-7 . . . . Gen. William . . Business Car. . . Baggage . . . . . . D&RG 1880. . . . . D&RG 1886. . . . . . . Paycar "R"
      Jackson Palmer   D&RGW 1963   Business car B-7